LIST OF WELSH ENTRIES IN THE
MEMORANDA ROLLS 1282–1343

D1477370

List of Welsh Entries
in the Memoranda Rolls
1282-1343

Edited with an Introduction
by
NATALIE FRYDE

Published on behalf of the University of Wales Board of Celtic Studies

CARDIFF
UNIVERSITY OF WALES PRESS
1974

© *University of Wales Press, 1974*

ISBN 0 7083 0540 7

GWASANAETH LLYFRGELL

C L W Y D

LIBRARY SERVICE

CLASS No.
DOSBARTH RHIF

ACCESSION NUMBER
RHIF LLYFR
R 1053907 C

QUALITEX PRINTING LIMITED CARDIFF

PREFACE

THANKS to the work of the Board of Celtic Studies, the sources relating to the history of Wales in the Public Record Office are gradually being made more available, both in volumes in the History and Law series and piecemeal in the History and Law section of the Bulletin of the Board.

The attempt to extend this work to the Exchequer class of the Medieval period is largely a new venture and presents the problem of dealing, not with a series of letters, all intrinsically interesting, but with a mass of routine business, scattered, unlisted, through a large number of bulky rolls. Mr. R. Latham's Calendar of the two Memoranda Rolls for the single regnal year 20 Edward II and 1 Edward III (1326–7) comprises 372 large pages and a full calendar of the Welsh material for the sixty years which constitute our period would obviously entail a considerable number of volumes and several more years of work, which the routine nature of some of this evidence would not justify. This list, therefore, is intended to indicate exactly where the Welsh entries are and what each entry is about, including more detail in the case of the more important and non-routine entries.

In all cases, except where otherwise stated, the Lord Treasurer's Remembrancer's Memoranda Roll (E.368) has been used as the basic source with cross references, entry by entry, to identical or closely connected entries on the King's Remembrancer's Roll (E.159). The additional K.R. entries which do not correspond with anything on the L.T.R. roll follow at the end of each year. In the section of Brevia directa Baronibus dates of royal writs are given. The majority are writs under the Great Seal unless otherwise stated. Cross reference is also made to closely connected business, though I have used this sparingly. In addition, in the case of the views and audits of accounts of the Chamberlains of North and South Wales I have included at the end of each entry a reference to the particulars of the account (chiefly to the Ministers' Accounts, S.C.6) and to the Enrolled Accounts (chiefly on the Pipe Rolls, E.372) in so far as they exist. Similar references have been added, where practicable, in the case of some other audits of accounts. As far as names of persons and places are concerned, I have left them in the original form if the modern form seemed at all doubtful. Place-names which it is impossible to identify have been put between inverted commas.

ACKNOWLEDGEMENTS

I SHOULD like to thank the staff of the Public Record Office for heaving these heavy rolls around for me, and also for allowing me to have out at once a large number of detailed accounts for the purpose of cross references. I should particularly like to thank Dr. Ralph Griffiths, of University College, Swansea, for his advice and also for lending me parts of his forthcoming volume on South Wales officials. I should also like to thank his collaborator, Dr. Roger Thomas, with whom I have discussed the work often. I am indebted to Dr. Dafydd Jenkins of the Law Department at Aberystwyth, who has given me a good deal of help with Welsh names, and I could not have done without the encouragement of Professor Glanmor Williams and Sir Goronwy Edwards.

CONTENTS

LIST OF ABBREVIATIONS

Advent. Vic.	Adventus Vicecomitum.
B.B.C.S.	Bulletin of the Board of Celtic Studies.
B.I.H.R.	Bulletin of the Institute of Historical Research.
Br. d. Bar.	Brevia directa Baronibus.
Br. Irr.	Brevia Irretornabilia.
Br. Ret.	Brevia Retornabilia.
C.A.C.	J. G. Edwards (ed.), *Calendar of Ancient Correspondence concerning Wales* (1935).
C.Cl.R.	Calendar of Close Rolls.
C.P.R.	Calendar of Patent Rolls.
Comm.	Commissiones et Littere Patentes.
D.d.	Dies Dati, Presentaciones, Attornati et Respectus.
E.H.R.	English Historical Review.
Fines	Fines, Manucaptiones, Redditus, Affidationes et Visores.
Hil.	Hilary Term.
K.R.	King's Remembrancer.
Latham	R. C. Latham, *Calendar of Memoranda Rolls 1326–27* (H.M.S.O., 1968).
L.T.R.	Lord Treasurer's Remembrancer.
Mich.	Michaelmas Term.
Pascha	Easter Term.
Prec. super Comp.	Precepta super Compotum.
Recogn.	Recogniciones.
St. et Vis.	Status et Visus Compotorum.
Trans. Cymm.	*The Transactions of the Honourable Society of Cymmrodorion.*
Trin.	Trinity Term.

INTRODUCTION

'IN range, diversity of content, comprehensiveness and interest the Memoranda Rolls of the Exchequer form the most important classes of records of that department . . . Certainly from about the middle of the reign of Edward I, if not before, the Memoranda Rolls are incomparably the classes of Exchequer records which give the most complete view of the whole of the Exchequer organisation and business, on the financial, administrative, and judicial sides.'[1] These comments of the late Dr. J. Conway Davies refer especially to the period after 1294, a decade after the beginning of our list, and, as he also noted, 'after the conquest of Wales the administration of the principality, in North and South or West Wales, is as clearly surveyed as the administration of England'.[2]

The Memoranda Rolls were annually compiled by the two Remembrancers of the Exchequer, one of whom, the King's Remembrancer, was a royal nominee, while his colleague was the personal clerk of the Lord Treasurer. This accounts for some of the main differences in the business recorded on their respective rolls, which will be discussed more fully later. The Remembrancers were not merely clerks, but acted, in practice, as heads of two important sub-departments of the Exchequer and ranked in status immediately after its Barons. When in January 1341 three new Barons had to be appointed to replace officials summarily dismissed by the King, two of the vacancies were filled by the two Remembrancers, Gervase Wilford and William Brocklesby.[3] The Remembrancers acted as important executive officials. They had to ensure that the Exchequer discharged all its normal tasks. It was their duty to make certain that all the mandates addressed by the King to the Exchequer were properly implemented, that all the persons who were summoned to the Exchequer duly appeared and did what was required of them, that all the decisions arising out of the accounting or out of other proceedings at the Exchequer were followed up by appropriate action. Hence arose the need to keep all the information required for the transaction of the current Exchequer business or deserving of permanent record for future reference. The Remembrancers, therefore, kept voluminous files of original documents[4] and also compiled memoranda about all the business that they had to supervise. It is these memoranda that were ultimately joined together to form the two annual Memoranda

---

[1] J. Conway Davies, 'The Memoranda Rolls of the Exchequer to 1307', *Studies Presented to Sir Hilary Jenkinson* (ed. J. Conway Davies, O.U.P., 1957), p. 97.

[2] *Ibid*, p. 152.

[3] *C.P.R. 1340–3*, p. 80 (20 January 1341).

[4] Some of them are preserved today in the modern P.R.O. classes of Brevia Baronibus (E.208), Bille (E.207) and Extents and Inquisitions (E.143), this last class constituting, in fact, a series of Exchequer mandates with returns to them.

Rolls, one for each Remembrancer, though a few of the original documents from files were also occasionally attached to these rolls.[5]

Until the last decade of the thirteenth century the bulk of the business supervised by the Remembrancers arose out of the activities of sheriffs and other collectors of regular royal revenues. After the conquest of North Wales the newly created Chamberlains of Caernarvon were naturally fitted into this system, though as it happens, the first important entries concerning the auditing of their accounts do not appear on the Memoranda Rolls until 1291 (nos. 46, 48). In the earlier years of Edward I the other main concern of the Remembrancers was with revenue-spending officials and with crown debtors in general. From the start of our list there are numerous entries connected with the expenditure on the building of the Welsh castles. These early rolls are relatively small. Until the 1290 ties they consist of fewer than fifty membranes and there was no need for any elaborate sub-dividing. An all-embracing section of 'communia' covered diverse things that will be divided into several distinct categories later on. For these reasons until 1295 we have only given membrane references,[6] as the headings of sub-sections are not very informative before that time.

Edward I was in France from 1286 to 1289. He incurred heavy debts and after his return from abroad he became aware of a weakening of his royal authority. He took vigorous fiscal and political measures to remedy this, which are amply reflected in the Memoranda Rolls. Some of the repercussions of this on his relations with the Welsh Marcher lords can be seen in a number of instances. In each case noted here friction arose over an attempt to increase revenue at the expense of local rights. This is particularly so in the case of the opposition of Edmund Mortimer to the collection of taxes by ordinary royal officials from his Welsh tenants in his Marcher lordships (nos. 68, 196). In 1292–4 William de Braose denied the King's right to collect a debt from Braose's Welsh tenants in Gower on the ground that writs of the Exchequer were not returnable from the Welsh Marcher lordships. Finally, there is also the enquiry into John Giffard's precise rights in his commote of Is Cennen. This arose out of a dispute over the types of cases in which a holder by barony in the county of Carmarthen was subject to the jurisdiction of the County Court (nos. 62, 65).

In the summer of 1294 Edward was forced into a war with France followed by a Welsh uprising at Michaelmas. This started a succession of emergencies that plagued Edward I for the remainder of his reign, and the balance of the Memoranda Rolls is quite changed by them. The transporting of troops and provisions to Welsh castles is stepped up and castles damaged

---

[5] The best modern accounts of the duties of the Remembrancers, and of the Memoranda Rolls in our period, are by J. F. Willard, 'The Memoranda Rolls and the Remembrancers, 1282–1350', *Essays in Medieval History presented to Thomas Frederick Tout* (ed. A. G. Little and F. M. Powicke, Manchester, 1925), pp. 215–29, and by J. Conway Davies, *loc. cit.*, pp. 97–154. See also E. B. Fryde, 'Materials for the Study of Edward III's Credit Operations, 1327–48', *B.I.H.R.*, 23 (1950), pp. 13–15, and R. C. Latham's introduction to his *Calendar of Memoranda Rolls (Exchequer), Michaelmas 1326–Michaelmas 1327* (H.M.S.O., 1968), cited hereafter as *Latham*.

[6] Nos. 1–72.

by the Welsh had to be repaired (no. 113). There are references to destruction of official records by the rebels, and this was presumably the reason why the Chamberlain of North Wales was unable to render account for the period from Michaelmas 1294 to July 1295 (nos. 94, 166).

The war of 1294–5 led to the taking of numerous Welsh hostages who were temporarily imprisoned in various English castles. These people must be clearly distinguished from the more permanently detained Welsh prisoners who at various times had been removed into England.

After the conquest of Wales in 1282–3, Gwenllian, daughter of Llywelyn ap Gruffydd and Eleanor de Montfort, was taken as a baby back to England and forced later to become a nun at Sempringham. Even into Edward III's reign she is receiving an assignment on the county of Lincoln to help with her maintenance at Sempringham.[7] Owen, son of Dafydd ap Gruffydd, her first cousin, was less fortunate in being a prisoner in Gloucester castle.[8]

Shortly after Llywelyn's last war we hear of two other prisoners, Rhys ap Maelgwn and Cynan ap Maredudd, two Cardiganshire chieftains,[9] who, after various changes of allegiance, were imprisoned at Bridgnorth castle.[10] After 1290 we find that they had been transferred to Northumberland where they were moved between Bamburgh and Newcastle on Tyne.[11] After 1295 we find imprisoned with them one Maelgwn ap Rhys, who may be the ally of Madog ap Llywelyn in West Wales.[12] Rhys and Cynan were released in 1297 and served the King of England in Flanders 'mounted on sorry nags'.[13] Their former companion, Maelgwn, was still imprisoned in Newcastle on Tyne in 1301.

The Rhys ap Maelgwn of the Flanders campaign should not be confused with the prisoner of the same name detained in Norwich castle where he was kept with his brother Gruffydd and another Rhys, the son of Rhys ap Maredudd.[14] Rhys ap Maelgwn and his brother Gruffydd were the direct descendants of the princely house of Deheubarth,[15] and were still boys when they were captured in West Wales and taken to Bristol, whence they passed into the custody of the sheriff of Norfolk.[16] They were still prisoners in Norwich castle in Edward II's reign,[17] though Rhys, the son of Rhys ap Maredudd, by September 1300 had been transferred to Windsor.[18]

---

[7] *Infra*, No. 591 (2 Edward III).

[8] *D.W.B.*, p. 94, Dafydd ap Gruffydd; E.368/68, m.17d., Pascha.

[9] Morris, *Welsh Wars of Edward I* (1901), p. 154.

[10] *C.A.C.*, p. 46.

[11] E.368/65, m.18.

[12] E.368/9, m.88d. He was perhaps not killed contrary to *D.W.B.*, followed by *Book of Prests* (ed. E. B. Fryde, 1962), p. xliii.

[13] Morris, p. 279.

[14] *C.Cl.R.* (*1288–96*), p. 493; E.159/75, m.84.

[15] *Handbook of British Chronology* (ed. F. M. Powicke and E. B. Fryde, 1961), p. 51.

[16] E.368/72, m.90d; E.368/76, m.84d; E.368/77, m.53.

[17] *Book of Prests*, p. xliii. *Infra*, no. 367 (11 Edward II).

[18] E.159/79, m.5d.

In their turn the sons of Madog ap Llywelyn were captured and spent a considerable part of their youth in English castles. We first have a payment for them on 11 June 1295 when they were in prison in Hereford castle at the same time as a number of Anglesey hostages.[19] They were still there in 1304.[20] By 1311 they had been transferred to the Tower of London.[21]

In 1295 by far the largest number of incumbents of English prisons, however, were temporary hostages rather than long-term prisoners. We have no evidence that they were involved in direct action against Edward. They were more likely to have been important men in the community whose detention would act as a deterrent to revolt by others. The first group taken was from Anglesey and includes the descendants of Ednyfed Vychan. The writ ordering their despatch to Shrewsbury is dated 23 April 1295, six and a half weeks after the battle of Maes Madog and some three months earlier than the instructions for dealing with hostages taken from the rest of Wales.[22] It would seem to have been executed while Edward himself was in Anglesey. They were all taken initially to Shrewsbury. Einion ap Madog ap Gadyn (who died soon after), Tegwared Du ap Bleddyn, Maredudd ap Llywelyn, Iorwerth Du ap Madog, Llywelyn Foel ap Einion ap Llywelyn, Goronwy ap Moelwar, Ednyfed ap Tegwared, Ednyfed ap Gruffydd and Hywel ap Ednyfed were kept at Shrewsbury until their release on 20 August 1296.[23] Another group was quickly transferred to Hereford: Hywel ap Gruffydd, Iorwerth ap Einion, Einion ap Madog, Maredudd ap Ednyfed and Meirig ap Madog. They were freed a week after their associates at Shrewsbury.[24] The remaining group were moved from Shrewsbury further south to St. Briavel's castle in Gloucestershire: Llywelyn Foelron, Howelinus ap Bleddyn, Iorwerth Vaughan ap Iorwerth ap Howel, David Michel, Ieuan Foel ('Le Ringold') and David Foel. They were released on 25 August.[25]

In 1295, besides the hostages from Anglesey, an additional 236 hostages were taken. Those of North Wales seem to have been assembled at Conway and then despatched to Chester.[26] Those of South Wales seem to have been despatched from Carmarthen to Bristol.[27] We cannot be certain when they were originally taken, but it would seem to be after the revolt had been largely defeated and Edward probably wanted them as surety for quiet in Wales as he intensified his war against France in Gascony and at sea.[28]

Of the 156 hostages from North Wales assembled at Chester under Reginald Grey, twenty-one remained there and the rest were sent to Nottingham. Seventy-five in turn were sent from Nottingham to York

19 E.368/67, m.70d.
20 E.368/75, m.86.
21 E.368/82, m.146d.
22 *C.Cl.R.* (*1288–96*), p. 425.
23 E.368/68, m.8d; E.159/69, m.54.
24 E.368/67, m.70d; E.368/68, m.75d.
25 E.368/68, m.47.
26 C.81/1700, no. 1; *C.Cl.R.* (*1288–96*), p. 425.
27 *Book of Prests*, p. xlv.
28 *Ibid*, p. xlvi.

where ten remained. The rest were despatched to Richmond (ten), Skipton in Craven (ten), Scarborough (twelve), Carlisle (twelve) and Newcastle on Tyne (twenty-one). They were freed on 9 September 1296.[29] The fifteen who were sent to Lincoln remained there until the end of July 1296.[30] The thirty who were sent to Leicester were subsequently placed in the custody of the sheriff of Northampton and divided equally between the castles of Oxford and Northampton.[31]

The order for dealing with the South Walian hostages was despatched on 26 August 1295.[32] They were sent by ship to Bristol, and the sheriffs of Dorset and Wiltshire had come there to escort them to the castles chosen for their safe-keeping. Of the fifty entrusted to the sheriff of Wiltshire ten were placed in Salisbury, ten in Marlborough and thirty in Winchester, whence ten were moved to Pevensey.[33] The sheriff of Dorset kept ten in Sherborne and twenty in the great castle of Corfe.[34]

After this, as far as we know, English prisons remained empty of Welsh hostages until the revolt of Llywelyn Bren in Glamorgan in 1315. Thirty-three North Wales hostages were kept at Chester from 29 August 1315 and remained there until 18 October 1317, during which time one of them died. Payments to them for their keep were made through Einion ap Philip, Cynfrig ap Philip, Tudur Gam and David ap Howel.[35]

The attempts made by Edward I to tax Wales are well documented in the Memoranda Rolls as are the opposition and rebellion which these taxes helped to provoke. Edward strained every resource at his disposal. It was not surprising that a number of innovations in his attempts to increase revenue occurred: the conquest of Wales made possible one of these, namely the extension of taxation to that country.

Edward first attempted this in 1291 when a request was made to the commonalty of Wales 'to grant a Fifteenth like the rest of the realm to meet the debts incurred in rescuing the King of Sicily'.[36] Edward's relations with his Marcher lords were poor in any case at this time, and it is not surprising that there was opposition to attempts to extend taxation amongst their tenantry in Wales. Roger Mohaut obtained an enrolment on the Patent Roll to the effect that the grants made by his tenants in Mold and Hawarden in Wales should not be regarded as a precedent.[37] Edmund Mortimer obtained the same enrolment but only after he had put up a spirited resistance to the King.[38] He prevented the Shropshire tax collectors from extending their activities to his Welsh lands at Wigmore. To him any tenant not answerable to the Justices Itinerant was outside the jurisdiction of English officials and could not be subjected to English taxation. He would grant the

---

[29] E.368/67, m.73; E.368/68, m.78d.
[30] E.159/70, m.34.
[31] E.368/67, m.70; E.368/68, m.75; E.159/69, mm.8, 56.
[32] C.Cl.R. (1288–96), p. 430.
[33] E.368/67, m.71; E.368/68, mm.17d, 73.
[34] E.368/67, m.73d.
[35] Infra, nos. 376, 398.
[36] C.P.R. (1281–92), p. 419.
[37] C.P.R. (1292–1301), p. 52.
[38] Ibid, p. 56.

Fifteenth from his Welsh lands only under the very special circumstances of special collectors being appointed for the Welsh lands.[39] Some £1,741 15s. 5¼d. was collected in Wales,[40] but one wonders if it can have been worth it since it can only have increased the tension in the very same areas of North-East Wales where the revolt of Madog ap Llywelyn was to break out next year. It may, to judge by the plea of Patrick Haselwell, Collector in Flint, have been a contributing factor. He said that he and his colleagues levied a part of the tax 'and then the war broke out on the morrow of Michaelmas and they could not levy even a quarter of the Fifteenth and *dared not*. After this time they levied nothing because many of the assessed were killed and others had very little left.'[41]

Nevertheless, when in 1300 Edward was embarking on another Scottish campaign and was sufficiently desperate for money, he made another attempt to tax Wales. In fact there were two separate taxes, one for Wales,[42] and a separate one for the Welsh tenants in the Marches.[43] We have a total of £2,776 13s. 4d. from Wales,[44] a considerable sum of money, though there was obviously some delay in collecting it, at least to judge from the King's desperate pleas to the commonalty of North Wales. £4,000 of the Fifteenth expected from the Marcher Tax was assigned to Welsh footsoldiers fighting in Scotland, though they may never have received much of it as the collectors were imprisoned for heavy arrears.[45]

Following the precedent of his father, in 1318 Edward II obtained a grant of a Fifteenth from North Wales.[46] It is perhaps indicative of the dissatisfaction with Edward II's policies in Wales, where the rebellion of Llywelyn Bren had just taken place, that comparatively little was collected. Only £929 12s. 9½d. is recorded as having been received as opposed to £1,333 6s. 8d. in Edward I's reign.[47] Edmund Dynieton, the Chamberlain of North Wales, received all but a few shillings. £100 of it was paid to Roger Mortimer of Chirk, Justice of Wales, going to Scotland, and 400 m. to Roger Mortimer of Wigmore in Ireland. £284 7s. 1d. was paid to the new Chamberlain, Henry Shirokes, presumably for the very large expenses on Welsh castles.[48] This 1318 tax seems to be the last one collected from Wales in Edward II's reign.

---

[39] *Infra*, no. 68.
[40] See Table I, *infra*.
[41] *Infra*, no. 167.
[42] Wales; *C.P.R. (1292–1301)*, p. 526.
[43] The March: *ibid*, p. 517.
[44] See Table II, *infra*.
[45] *Infra*, nos. 191, 202.
[46] *C.A.C.*, p. 179; *C.P.R. (1317–21)*, pp. 242–3.
[47] See Table II, *infra*.
[48] *Supra*, no. 398.

Table I
All the references are to P.R.O. mss.

Taxacio Wallencium, 1293

	£.	s.	d.	
Lands of Hugh Mortimer	172.	12.	1¾.	E.179/242/57
Merioneth	667.	13.	5¼.	*Ibid* 58
Flint	464.	17.	0¾.	E.372/140, m.48
Nevin and Dinllaen	6.	16.	0½.	E.179/242/50b
Creuddyn	3.	15.	0.	*Ibid* 51
Commitmaen	111.	18.	8½.	*Ibid* 58
Is Cennen, Bronllys, Glasbury (lands of John Giffard)	44.	10.	6½.	*Ibid* 60
Lands of Roger Mortimer in Powys	67.	7.	0.	*Ibid* 55
Lands of William fil' Griffin de la Pole (Keneylor, Arwystli, La Pole)	202.	5.	6.	E.179/242/54
Total	1,741.	15.	5¼.	

This total is, apparently, only a fraction of what was collected, but it is useful as giving us a minimum figure.

Table II

Taxacio Wallencium, 1300   E.372/150, m.43d.
Compotus Ricardi Havering, clerici, de subsidio per communitatem Wallie . . . in subsidium guerre sue Scocie concesso, anno 28.

	£.	s.	d.
North Wales	1,333.	6.	8.
West Wales	733.	6.	8.
Flint	333.	6.	8.
Powys	266.	13.	4.
Builth	50.		
Montgomery	60.		
Total	£2,776.	13.	4.

Fifteenth, 1318   E.359/14, m.13d.
Compotus Edmundi Dynieton, collectoris quintedecime a militibus et probis hominibus ac etiam de tota communitate parcium illarum de bonis suis mobilibus pro expeditione guerre sue Scocie anno 12 levande, prout alias fieri consueverunt . . .

	£.	s.	d.
Caernarvon county	377.	10.	4¼d.
Anglesey ,,	325.	5.	2.
Merioneth	226.	17.	3¼d.
Total	£929.	12.	9½d.

The rising of 1294–5 also affected adversely the levies of clerical taxes. Far into the reign of Edward II the Exchequer was inquiring in vain into the arrears of a tax from the laity in Flintshire (no. 167) and of the clerical levies in the dioceses of both North and South Wales. The Prior of Llanthony actually claimed that any attempt by him to levy the clerical tax of 1294 in the diocese of St. David's would have provoked the burning of the properties pertaining to his benefices (nos. 315, 363). These Exchequer enquiries give us an interesting body of evidence about the devastation caused by the rising and the consequent impoverishment (e.g. nos. 412, 420 in the diocese of Bangor). In the last decade of the reign the Scottish wars loom large in the rolls and payments to contingents of Welsh troops serving against the Scots recur frequently, as they will continue to do in the reign of Edward II.

The enormous expansion in the amount of business handled by the Exchequer on account of these recurrent emergencies forced the Remembrancers to sub-divide these records much more elaborately, and they also began to seek ways of avoiding excessive duplication of notes. The decisive changes in the composition of the rolls occurred between 1294 and 1307, though further experiments took place also under Edward II. By 1323 the Remembrancers have evolved a reasonably satisfactory system of arranging the rolls and it was made permanent by the Exchequer Ordinance of that year.[49]

After 1290 several new types of fiscal business for the first time came permanently under the control of the Exchequer. In that year its officials first began to supervise in detail the collection of direct taxes and the auditing of the accounts of the collectors.[50] In 1294 the revenue from the customs at all the main harbours, which had previously been administered by the King's bankers, the Riccardi of Lucca, came under the direct supervision of the Exchequer.[51] The addition of the taxes and the customs to the revenues controlled by the Exchequer led to the expansion of the practice of making assignments on future revenues by the sole authority of the Treasurer, using mandates under the Exchequer seal. Such mandates were recorded in a new section of the rolls, which first appears separately in 1296–7, under the heading of 'brevia irretornabilia',[52] that is mandates not requiring a reply.

These additions of the 1290 ties to the range of matters supervised by the Exchequer led to an increase in the number of Welsh entries on the Memoranda Rolls, though on a smaller scale than might have been expected. Several factors must be borne in mind. As far as the ordinary administration was concerned only the Chamberlains of North and South Wales and some of the keepers of castles had to account at Westminster. The Welsh sheriffs and other subordinate officials, unlike their English counterparts, were almost never summoned to appear at the Exchequer. Furthermore, if the subordinates of the Chamberlains owed money to them, the Exchequer normally left the Chamberlains to their own devices, and the officials at Westminster only very seldom took effective direct action in support of the Chamberlains. As for the extraordinary revenues from customs and taxes, Wales bore only a small proportion of these new burdens. There were

[49] H. Hall, *The Red Book of the Exchequer*, III (R.S., 1896), pp. 863–87.
[50] J. F. Willard, *Parliamentary Taxes on Personal Property, 1290 to 1334* (Cambridge, Mass., 1934), p. 9, and, for more details, chapters X–XI.
[51] Cf. *Revue Belge de Philologie et d'Histoire*, xl (1962), pp. 1175, 1179–81, based mainly on the Memoranda Rolls.
[52] Conway Davies, *loc. cit.*, p. 116.

Welsh collectors of customs at Haverfordwest, and the auditing of their account is first mentioned in 1299 (no. 162), but the amounts levied by them were always slight. As we have already noted, Edward I had first tried to tax his Welsh subjects in 1291, but the Welsh uprising of 1294–5 seriously interfered with the levy of lay and clerical taxes in Wales. The lay taxes of 1300 and 1318 did not yield much. All the clerical taxes contributed by the English clergy were also collected in the Welsh dioceses, but the amounts were small and seldom occasioned serious problems.

In the reign of Edward II the recurrent political crises led to an expansion of the 'extraordinary' business of the Exchequer and the growth of the rolls to a size where, by the end of the reign, they become quite difficult to lift. An important point to be made is that the disorder in the realm at no time led to the breakdown of the Exchequer, where, on the contrary, the rolls are becoming more and more comprehensive, the writs more businesslike and stereotyped and the Barons more exacting. There is a new preoccupation with the exaction of arrears from all officials, though whether this is a reflection of the greater disorder in the country or the new efficiency in the Exchequer, it is difficult to say.

For Edward II's reign the rolls are not so much interesting as invaluable. The aftermath of the death at Bannockburn of the young Earl of Gloucester, who was lord of Glamorgan, in 1314, that is the rising of Llywelyn Bren and the growing influence of the Despensers, is clearly reflected in them. The King demanded a fine from the men of Glamorgan as punishment for the rebellion. The money was to be used, ostensibly, for the Scottish war (nos. 317, 324), but it soon found its way into the young Despenser's pocket (no. 352). There is a petition about the maltreatment of hostages taken from Glamorgan (no. 326) and also, as noted above, references to the fact that hostages were taken from North Wales, although, as far as we know, there was no rising there (nos. 376, 398). There are audits of the accounts of the custodians of Glamorgan before it was granted to the younger Despenser, who later instigated proceedings against two of them. In one of these cases, the accounts of the widow of Payn Turbervill', the former custodian, were sent to Despenser for examination, though proceedings appear to have ended on Despenser's failure to send a return to the Exchequer (no. 365). Despenser was similarly commissioned to investigate the administration of Glamorgan by John Giffard of Brimpsfield, another former custodian (nos. 373, 430), who was one of the enemies of the Despensers executed in 1322.

The audits of Chamberlains' accounts are useful for details of military activities both in the crisis which followed Despenser's return from exile late in 1321 and in that of 1326. This evidence confirms the discovery of Sir Goronwy Edwards that there existed a strong body of Welsh partisans of Edward II.[53] In 1321–2 Rhys ap Gruffydd, a relative of Gruffydd Llwyd, is paid for having marched with a huge force of 3,000 infantry and 40 men-

---

[53] J. G. Edwards, 'Sir Gruffydd Llwyd', E.H.R., XXX (1915), pp. 589–601. Our rolls contain a reference to a detention of Gruffydd Llwyd by the Justice of Wales, Roger Mortimer of Chirk, at some unspecified date in 1317–19 (cf. no. 398).

at-arms into Cantref Mawr, Cantref Bychan and other parts of South-West Wales to seize the lands of Edward's opponents (no. 467). In 1326 he was again relied upon to stand by the King. There is a reference to a very important mandate under the privy seal of 11 October addressed to Rhys. It was sent from Gloucester during Edward's flight westwards, and it ordered Rhys to come to the King with as large a contingent of all kinds of troops as possible. Rhys received the large sum of £259 2s. 8d. from the Chamberlains of South Wales for wages of his men during eight days while conducting them to Brecon (no. 593). The mystery is why they never effectively helped Edward to mount resistance in Wales to the King's enemies, Queen Isabella and Roger Mortimer. All that we know is that Rhys was forced to flee to Scotland and then to seek a pardon from the new English government.[54] Edward II certainly had enemies as well as friends in Wales. Robert Power, the Chamberlain of North Wales, turned against him in the crisis of 1326. In 1331 this official was granted a huge reward of £300 for assuring the keeping of North Wales 'at the time of the pursuing of Hugh Despenser' (no. 692).

These are important people and great events. As far as ordinary people in Wales are concerned, there are only scattered fragments to be noticed, and we must endorse Sir David Evans' view that the records of the English royal administration 'illustrate the working of the government of the Principality, for they were made by officials for the information of other officials. But the activities of the governed are described from the point of view of the governors and a study based almost entirely on records must of necessity have an administrative bias.'[55] There are a number of lists of Welsh tenants (e.g. no. 194, in Archenfield) and some valuable lists of local officials (e.g. no. 580, in South-West Wales in 1321–5), but we have lost our most useful source for officialdom and government on a lower level with the loss of the records that may once have been kept at Caernarvon and Carmarthen. Only when the Chamberlains in their accounting at the Exchequer tried to secure allowances for some Welsh customary rents or other exactions that could not be collected do we get more detailed glimpses of local Welsh arrangements. One such claim concerned the free tenants of the commote of Ardudwy in Merioneth who had been deprived of an office by the royal bailiffs and were refusing to pay the annual rent that they owed for it (no. 564). Much more serious was the complaint of the villeins of Penrhos in Anglesey that in the extent of their manor made by the officials of Edward I after his conquest of Wales they had been erroneously surcharged. In their petition to the King they described the extent as 'unreasonable' and assessed the annual surcharge at over £21. One of the Chamberlains who had claimed allowance for this exaction alleged that if an attempt was made to levy this rent the King would lose all his villeins at Penrhos (nos. 456, 563, 680).

[54] *Trans. Cymm.*, 1913–14, p. 195.

[55] 'Some notes on the History of the Principality of Wales, 1343–1376', *ibid*, 1925–6, p. 27.

Welsh entries might be found in every section of the Memoranda Rolls and all these subdivisions will need to be discussed, though some deserve only the briefest of mentions. Two subdivisions provide the agenda for the Exchequer's dealings with the sheriffs and are a survival of its main original function. This does concern us, as the English sheriffs sometimes made payments connected with happenings in Wales. 'The coming of the sheriffs' ('adventus vicecomitum') recorded the actual appearances at the Exchequer of these officials together with mentions of money, warrants and vouchers that they had brought with them. 'The days given to the sheriffs' ('dies dati vicecomitibus') listed the dates assigned for their attendance at the Exchequer. Mandates and petitions sent to the Exchequer were kept on files. Those that came from the King were also normally copied on the Memoranda Rolls. It was the special task of the King's Remembrancer to ensure that the royal mandates were carried out. His enrolments of them, therefore, often contain additional notes about the further execution of these royal orders. This section of 'writs directed to the Barons of the Exchequer' ('brevia directa baronibus') became so voluminous that the framers of the Exchequer Ordinance of 1323 ordered that it should be confined to only one of the two rolls, naturally, the K.R. roll.

The majority of these writs emanated from the chancery, though Mr. Latham has estimated that rather over 10 per cent of those in the roll for 1326–7 were mandates under the Privy Seal.[56] In the reign of Edward III some writs under the Chamber seals were also enrolled, including a few from Wales. As we no longer possess the registers of either the writs of the Privy Seal or of the Chamber seals, the enrolments on the Memoranda Rolls provide our only known texts of these particular mandates. This is also true, however, of a considerable proportion of the mandates under the Great Seal addressed to the Exchequer. As Mr. Latham has pointed out, of the writs of this sort enrolled on the roll for 1326–7, fewer than a quarter can be traced on the Close Rolls of the Chancery. Some of the others can be found on other types of Chancery Rolls (e.g. Liberate Rolls and Fine Rolls) but an appreciable number cannot now be traced on any of the existing series of Chancery enrolments. It should be remembered, however, that the officials of the Chancery had an alternative method of keeping a record of the mandates which were sent out of the Chancery, by filing drafts or copies among the Chancery files, of which only a mere remnant can now be identified.

One final comment must be added about the handling of royal mandates by the Exchequer. If they were sent directly to the King they would normally be enrolled on the Memoranda Rolls shortly after they had been issued. But many of these mandates merely conferred favours on some particular persons, and it was the business of each beneficiary to produce them at the Exchequer, which might happen only after a considerable lapse of time. Hence the writs enrolled during any particular Exchequer term differ widely in dates and do not follow each other in any chronological order.

---

56 Cf. his introduction to the 'writs addressed to the barons', *op. cit.*, pp. xiii-xv.

The miscellaneous section of 'the records' ('recorda') is of great interest to historians. It contains summaries of all the special proceedings, including trials, before the Treasurer and Barons of the Exchequer. Originals or copies of petitions, of records of enquiries and of other documents were often included here. Some of the entries occur on both rolls, but the divergent preoccupations of the two Remembrancers are particularly in evidence here. The King's Remembrancer was especially concerned with the non-routine matters, including things arising out of the enforcement of the King's authority. Occasional sources of income, such as reliefs due from the new tenants-in-chief, and other incidents of feudal tenure, were particularly within his province. An interesting example, already mentioned before in another context, is provided by the proceedings in 1292–4 concerning debts owed by the Braose family for reliefs, fines for marriage and other liabilities (no. 59). This case, as has been noted before, had important political implications, as it involved the claim of the Exchequer to collect debts wihin the Marcher lordship of Gower. Some of these proceedings are entered on both the rolls, but the record on the K.R. roll is much fuller, and it is only here that we find notes about further proceedings that dragged on until at least 1302.

The two Remembrancers shared a common interest in the auditing of accounts, but here also each had some special functions. Some of the resultant transactions were noted among 'records', but there are also two other sections specially devoted to accounting. 'Precepts' ('precepta') contained a summary of the instructions given to the English sheriffs during their appearances at the Exchequer and they concern Wales only occasionally, as, for example, over the custody of the Welsh hostages (cf. *supra*). The 'state and view of accounts' ('status et visus compotorum') is one of our most important sources. Both here and in the 'records', the King's Remembrancer was specially concerned with the initial stages of bringing to the Exchequer the persons who were required to render accounts and of conducting a preliminary 'view' of their liabilities. Once the stage of the final audit was reached, the Lord Treasurer's Remembrancer took over. He was particularly concerned with the exaction of arrears that still remained due to the Crown after an account had been rendered. It was also a part of his duties to supervise the collection of the ordinary royal revenues and to deal with officials who had to account regularly. A considerable proportion of the entries concerned with the Welsh Chamberlains are to be found only on L.T.R. rolls, or, at least, are more fully recorded there.

Two subsections of 'communia' included under multiple headings entries dealing with a variety of business subsidiary to accounting. One of these groups of entries includes 'days given' ('dies dati'), recording dates assigned to persons other than sheriffs for their appearance at the Exchequer. The other of these two subsections is headed by the word 'fines', the term used for financial settlements concluded by the King with royal debtors. This subsection also included sureties ('manucapciones') provided by persons accounting at the Exchequer as a guarantee that they would appear when required.

Yet another subsection dealing partly with matters subsidiary to accounting at the Exchequer are the 'recognizances' ('recogniciones') which first appeared on the rolls in 46–47 Henry III.[57] A recognizance normally stipulated a date when a debt was due to be paid and, in the case of default, it was automatically enforceable by the Exchequer. These recognizances might cover genuine debts due to the King, but they might represent instead special guarantees for the performance of some conditions imposed by the Crown. Private persons connected with the Exchequer, and influential notables, such as Hugh Despenser the Younger, also used these facilities for recording debts due to them, several Welshmen appearing among Despenser's debtors.

One of the most important functions of the Remembrancers was the recording of documents issued under the Exchequer seal. They are copied in several sections of the rolls. Very formal documents are grouped under the heading of 'commissions and letters patent'. Into this category came the letters of appointment ('commissiones') of various fiscal officials and the contracts for farming out royal estates or other crown assets. Mandates sent out by the Exchequer were known as 'writs on the King's behalf' ('brevia pro rege'). As we have already noted, they became subdivided into two categories. 'Non-returnable writs' were mandates to which no reply was required, consisting largely of assignments on future royal revenues. Some assignments were drawn on the Welsh revenues of the Crown. 'Returnable writs' ('brevia retornabilia') formed a much larger class. Each Remembrancer copied those 'returnable writs' that specially concerned him, and further notes were frequently added recording what happened subsequently.

The rolls furnish especially interesting information about the accounts of the Chamberlains of North and South Wales. The most detailed evidence is to be found in the views and audits of accounts. The distinction between these two types of entries reflects important differences of procedure. 'Views' are likely to be particularly detailed, but the figures in them are less definitive than in 'audits'. A view of account was merely a preliminary survey that might provide the Treasurer and Barons with a general impression of what was happening and give them an indication of outstanding problems. No attempt was apparently made to scrutinise closely each figure of revenue and expenditure. The Exchequer officials entrusted with the view similarly do not seem to have been empowered to pronounce definitively about the validity of the vouchers and warrants submitted to them.[58] In the case of the Chamberlains there existed diverse reasons for holding a view. It might be merely an interim report on activities that were still in progress. This is brought out particularly clearly in an entry concerning Thomas Cheddesworth, Chamberlain of North Wales, where a view and an audit are combined together. For the first two years of the tenure of his office (Michaelmas 1312–Michaelmas 1314) an audit was carried out late in 1314, resulting in a debt of £3,086, but it is followed by a view for a further period from Michaelmas 1314 to 5 January 1315, during which

57 J. Conway Davies, *loc. cit.*, p. 114.
58 *B.I.H.R.*, XXIII (1950, *cit. supra*), pp. 16–17.

time he had collected the additional comparatively paltry sum of £148 (no. 304). The Exchequer might be reduced to holding a view instead of an audit because the vouchers submitted by a Chamberlain were not complete enough or because he had spent money without having a proper warrant to do so.[59] On several occasions views had to be held instead of audits because the Controllers, who were both the colleagues of the Chamberlains and the deputies of the Justice of Wales, had failed to bring their counter-rolls to the Exchequer (e.g. nos. 303, 456, 753, 754). These counterrolls were regarded as quite indispensable for the holding of a final audit. They were supposed to corroborate all the information recorded on the Chamberlain's own rolls. Furthermore, the details of the judicial income arising out of the activities of the Justices were entered only on the counter-rolls.[60]

The audits of Chamberlains' accounts are usually copied on both the rolls, but the L.T.R. roll provides a fuller and more authoritative record, especially as notes about subsequent proceedings would normally only be added here. These audits can be divided for convenience into two main types. An audit might begin with a statement of the total amount charged to a Chamberlain, identical with what was charged to him in his Enrolled Account on the Pipe Roll (cf. no. 166; no. 559 and *Latham*, p. xxiv). Alternatively, the record of audit might have been made at a later stage of accounting, when a Chamberlain had already secured allowance for the bulk of his expenditure, so that the audit starts with only the statement of arrears due from him. An audit that begins with a small debt obviously belongs to the second category. There are also some complex cases that do not fall neatly into either of these categories and might necessitate a whole series of proceedings at the Exchequer[61] (e.g. nos. 433, 524, 527, concerning Henry Shirokes, Chamberlain of North Wales).

The financial fortunes of the Chamberlains varied immensely. Some managed to account quite satisfactorily, but a few were apparently ruined by their tenure of this office. Thomas Esthall's long series of tribulations will be discussed below. Adam Withiford died in December 1335 in the Tower of London, to which he had been committed for debts incurred as Chamberlain, in turn, of [both] North and, later, of South Wales (no. 753).

---

[59] Cf. *Latham* (*cit. supra*), p. xxiii.

[60] E.g. S.C.6/1219/14 is the roll of Robert, Prior of Carmarthen, Chamberlain of South Wales, Michaelmas 1320–Michaelmas 1321. It is crossed out, which shows that it was copied by the Engrosser of the Excheqer in writing out the Enrolled Account. It contains a note: 'De finibus et amerciamentis coram R. de Mortuo Mari, Justiciario Wallie et eciam coram R. de Malleye, locum eius tenente in partibus Suthwallie per totum annum presentem etc. 166 li. 17s. 9d.'.

The counter-roll (S.C.6/1219/13) is not crossed out. It contains a detailed list of amercements and of fines offered to the Justice, ending with the identical total of £166 17s. 9d. There are several more such pairs of rolls.

[61] Cf. the discussion of audits in *Latham*, p. xxiv.

The treatment meted out by the Exchequer to different Chamberlains cannot be explained by purely financial considerations. A few were clearly men of considerable importance, or else had influential patrons. Richard Abingdon, Chamberlain of Caernarvon (1284–6) became subsequently a Baron of the Exchequer,[62] and was employed in 1314 to examine the accounts of one of his successors, Thomas Esthall.[63] Hugh Leominster, Chamberlain of North Wales from July 1295 to 1301, was an especially important official. He had been connected for several years with the administration of the lands of Queen Eleanor in Wales, played an important part in the repression of the Welsh rising of 1294–5 and was appointed to the Chamberlainship at the end of this emergency to supervise the restoration of royal authority.[64] Robert Power, Chamberlain of North Wales from 1323 to October 1327, had earned the gratitude of the enemies of Edward II by turning against Edward during the latter's flight into Wales in October–November 1326. In 1331 the Exchequer recorded a royal gift to Power of £300 as a reward for his actions at this crucial moment (no. 692). When Power's accounts came up for final audit, the Exchequer was ordered to deal with him expeditiously as he was proceeding abroad in the King's service (no. 687). It is not surprising that all his claims for allowances were satisfactorily settled (nos. 651, 688). Nicholas Acton, who held the same office in 1329–30, secured similar favourable treatment, perhaps because he enjoyed the patronage of Thomas Beauchamp, Earl of Warwick. In August 1330 he was the earl's nominee for the office of one of the two Chamberlains of the Exchequer, which was in the hereditary gift of the earl's family no. 665). It was as a member of the Exchequer staff that Acton had his accounts audited by his new colleagues and he was able to secure a number of special royal mandates in his favour (nos. 680, 690–1).

Some Chamberlains encountered immense difficulties in getting their accounts accepted by the Exchequer and in clearing themselves of debt. The rolls supply only a partial explanation of the causes of these troubles, but we do get valuable glimpses of some of the things that could go wrong. The disobedience of the Welsh sheriffs and other subordinates of the Chamberlains was one perennial cause of trouble. A particularly serious breakdown of the Chamberlain's authority occurred in the last years of Edward II's reign in South-West Wales. Thomas Duyn, one of the two Chamberlains who acted jointly in 1321–6, complained bitterly of the fact that Edmund, Earl of Arundel, the Justice of Wales, and his deputy, Rhys ap Gruffydd, had appointed during these years numerous subordinate officials without the Chamberlain's consent. These nominees of the Justice failed to give Duyn accustomed pledges for behaving satisfactorily towards him. When, in April 1328, at the final audit of his accounts for 1321–5, Duyn was faced with the enormous debt of £472, he claimed that all the

---

[62] *C.Cl.R., 1302–7*, pp. 397–8.
[63] E.368/85, m.233d (summarised in no. 303).
[64] W. H. Waters, *The Edwardian Settlement of North Wales and its Administrative and Legal Aspects, 1284–1343* (Cardiff, 1935), p. 21; *Book of Prests of the King's Wardrobe for 1294–5 presented to John Goronwy Edwards* (ed. E. B. Fryde, Oxford, 1962), p. 249, index under Lememstr (Leominster), Hugh. His *Enrolled Account* as Chamberlain is published in *B.B.C.S.*, 15 (1953), pp. 126–56.

money was still in the hands of these defiant officials. The Exchequer enquiry which followed produced a long list of defaulters. In January 1330 Duyn still owed £115, and this remaining debt continued to be exacted as late as 1349 (no. 580).

As we have already mentioned, the Exchequer insisted that all the accounts of the Chamberlains must be compared with the counter-rolls of their Controllers. As we have seen, this was a justifiable requirement, but it could always become a potential source of delay and trouble. The Controllers were independent officials, acting as deputies of the Justices of Wales who appointed them. It was up to the Justices to ensure the presence of the Controllers at the Exchequer. The political upheavals of the years 1321–30 involved the sudden dismissals, and even executions, of several successive Justices, and this aggravated still further the problem of securing the attendance at the Exchequer of their erstwhile deputies. The prolonged tribulations of Thomas Esthall, extending over twenty years, provide a particularly well-documented example of what might happen. After acting as Chamberlain of North Wales from 1302 to 1312, Esthall was charged with a debt of £10,220 11s. 10d. It is possible that he may have been inefficient, but there is nothing to suggest that he was regarded as dishonest. A preliminary view of some of his accounts was held in November 1314, and he was then temporarily imprisoned. His lands, valued at £4 6s. 8d. a year, were taken into the King's hands and remained thus sequestrated until 1331. Further attempts to audit Esthall's account occurred in 1318, and in March 1330. On each occasion he was imprisoned for a while and then released on mainprise. Only after the overthrow of Roger Mortimer later that year, did the King at least take pity on this old royal servant. The Exchequer was ordered to investigate all the facts and to grant such allowances as justice demanded. Finally, the whole sorry tale emerged: one of the main causes of Esthall's troubles lay in the disappearance of the counter-rolls of the deputy of Hugh Audley the Elder, Justice between 1306 and 1308. These rolls had been accidentally burnt in a fire on one of Audley's manors, as Audley had duly certified the Exchequer, but its officials had persistently refused to take note of this disaster. The Audleys had been on the losing side in the civil war of 1321–2, the former Justice had died, while his son and heir—the Younger Hugh Audley—was imprisoned from 1322 to 1326. This may have contributed to Esthall's helplessness as long as Edward II ruled. After the audit of his account was finally completed in 1332, he was found to owe £1,690 15s., which Edward III graciously pardoned (nos. 303, 356, 377, 652, 681–4). More tragic still was the fate of Adam Withiford. He had acted as Chamberlain of North Wales from Easter 1330 to Easter 1331, and this proved his undoing. The first of the Justices under whom he had served, Roger Mortimer, Earl of March, was executed in November 1330, and Mortimer's successor, John Wysham, died in 1331. Withiford could never secure the production at the Exchequer of the counter-rolls of the deputies of these two Justices. He was presumably regarded as a satisfactory official, because in 1332–3 he was transferred to the Chamberlainship of South Wales. But in the summer of 1334 he was committed to the Tower of London. He was charged with a debt of £176, though if his counterclaims had been accepted he should have been completely cleared of all liability. His failure to produce the counter-rolls for 1330 was one of the reasons for his imprisonment, and he died in the Tower a year and a half later, in December 1335 (no. 753). There was something inhumanly bureaucratic in an Exchequer system that produced such results.

EDWARD I

E.368/56 10–11 Edward I (1282–3)

No. 1 (m.1), Mich.:
A day is given to Ithel fil' Oeli to render account for the annual rent of £100 which his father owed for Builth. (E.159/56, m.1, Mich.)

No. 2, *ibid*:
Allowance of £20 1s. is made to Gervase de Wileford, sheriff of Notts and Derby, because of his expense in sending 200 'compictores' from his bailiwick to Rhuddlan. (E.159/56, m.1, Mich.)

No. 3 (m.2), Hil.:
Memorandum that John Tydmarsh, sheriff of Oxon and Berks, had a day for account on the morrow of the Purification and did not appear because he was transporting victuals to Wales in the king's service. (E.159/56, m.2.)

No. 4 (m.14), Pascha:
Allowance to the sheriff of Lancashire for his expenses in sending 200 horsemen and 20 'cementarii' to Rhuddlan.

E.368/57 11–12 Edward I (1283–4)

No. 5 (m.1), Mich.:
Pardon to Roger Moeles of all arrears for the time he was a royal official in Wales. (Moeles was custodian of the castle of Llanbadarn Fawr.) *C.A.C.*, p. 45.

No. 6 (m.4d), Hil.:
The sheriff of Yorkshire is allowed £1 10s. for the expense of sending 20 'cementarii' to Rhuddlan.

No. 7 (m.7d), Pascha:
Allowance to the sheriff of Hereford for £10 paid to 100 'copiatores' sent from Hereford to Rhuddlan for their work for 8 days at 3d. a day; also for the expenses of 200 horsemen for 8 days; for 200 'copiatores' and carbonarii' sent to Brecon; £9 8s. for corn and oats sent from Hereford to Montgomery and there delivered to Grimbald Pauncefoot; and 40s. paid for the carriage of the 711m. 6s. 8d. conceded by the people of Hereford as a loan to the king and taken to the wardrobe at Chester. Also *infra*, m.26.

E.368/58   12–13 Edward I   (1284–5)

No. 8 (m.2d), Mich.:
The sheriff of Lancashire is to take into the king's hands all the lands of the late 'Wydo fil' Madock fil' Glevyn', enemy and rebel against the king, who was killed in the company of the king's enemies in the Welsh war. (E.159/58, m.1d., Mich.)

No. 9 (m.3), Mich.:
Record concerning a fine imposed on the men of 'Irchinfeld' (Archenfield) for illegal deforestation. (E.159/58, m.1d, Mich.)

No. 10, *ibid*:
The abbot of Hyde has delivered 100m. to William Perton, Custodian of Flint and Rhuddlan, for building operations and is quit of his debt to the king.

No. 11 (m.4), Mich.:
Respite in the arrears of his account allowed to the sheriff of Salop and Staffs because of his various expenses in the Welsh expedition.

No. 12 (m.4d), Mich.:
Assignment of the £2,000 owed to the king by the bishop of Winchester and the prior and convent of St. Swithun's, Winchester, to Richard Abingdon, chamberlain of North Wales, for building operations in castles. (E.159/58, m.4, Hil.) *C.Cl.R., 1279–88*, 2 January 1295, p. 309.

No. 13 (m.6), Hil.:
The Twentieth requested by the king from the clergy to meet the urgent need in facing the king's confederated enemies in Wales is to be brought to the Temple. (E.159/58, m.5d, Hil.)

No. 14 (m.11d), Trin.:
The barons of the Exchequer are to audit the account of John Radnor, custodian of the building operations at Builth from 13 January 1282 until the castle was handed over to Stephen Knoll. (E.159/58, m.9, Trin.)

No. 15 (m.27), Pascha:
The sheriff of Hereford is to distrain Llywelyn le Bret for 100s.

No. 16 (m.28), Pascha:
Allowance to the sheriff of Notts and Derby for carpenters and other workmen sent to Rhuddlan and Caernarvon, and for the expenses of Gruffydd ap Maredudd imprisoned in Nottingham castle.

E.159/58   12–13 Edward I   (1284–5)

No. 17 (m.2), Mich.:
Three Bristol burgesses who were at Caernarvon, 22 July 1284, and could not render account, are not to be distrained.

No. 18 (m.5), Hil.:
Allowance to the sheriff of Norfolk and Suffolk for the expense of sending two fishermen to Anglesey.

No. 19 (m.9d), Trin.:
Allowance to Bogo de Knovill', constable of Montgomery castle, in his rent of £78 9s. 11d. for the cost of a hall and a room constructed in the castle; allowance of £2 12s. 6d. paid to 100 foot soldiers sent from Montgomery to Caernarvon at 2d. a day, for three days.

E.368/59   13–14 Edward I   (1285–6)

No. 20 (m.4), Hil.:
Ralph Broughton has rendered account for the time he was custodian of building operations at Llanbadarn Fawr and receiver of money for the army in Wales, and is shown as quit in the account of William Louth, keeper of the Wardrobe. (E.159/59, m.18, Mich.) Cf. no. 45.

No. 21 (m.9), Pascha:
Walter Mauley is quit of his scutage for service in Wales which he paid to Thomas Bek, bishop of St. David's, keeper of the Wardrobe. (E.159/59, m.25, Pascha.)

No. 22 (m.11), Trin.:
Owen de la Pole, son of Gruffydd fil' Gwenynwyn, Fulk fitz Warin and Robert le Dus stand surety for the debts of the late Gruffydd fil' Gwenynwyn. (E.159/59, m.8d, Pascha.)

E.368/60   14–15 Edward I   (1286–7)

No. 23(m.1), Mich.:
Respite for Humphrey de Bohun, earl of Hereford, in the payment of his debts to the Exchequer because he has stayed in Wales to keep the peace. (E.159/60, m.1, Mich.)

No. 24 (m.2), *ibid*:
Writ to the barons of the Exchequer instructing them to find whether the free men of the lands of Owen fil' Gruffydd have been taxed. Endorsed that Henry Bray, escheator south of Trent, has exacted the Ninth from them.

No. 25 (m.4), Hil.:
The manor of Ashford (Kent), granted to Gruffydd ap Gwenynwyn and his heirs, has been taken back into the king's hands as he 'iam a fide nostra recessit' and is granted to Queen Eleanor.

No. 26 (m.5), Pascha; (m.6), Trin:
The executors of William Perton have respite in paying arrears owed by him as custodian of Flint castle. (E.159/60, m.6, Pascha.) Cf. no. 40. Enr. Acc. E.372/125, m.29.

E.159/60   14–15 Edward I   (1286–7)

No. 27 (m.6), Pascha:
The abbot of Pershore has delivered 20m. to the Keeper of the Wardrobe at Rhuddlan for his Welsh scutage and is quit. Cf. *infra*, m.17, Pascha.

No. 28 (m.8), Trin.:
Allowance made to Ralph Sandwich, constable of the Tower and of the castle of Devizes, of £34 for the expenses of Rhys Vychan and Llywelyn, his brother, in his custody until 13 April 1287.

L.T.R. rolls for 15–17 Edward I (1287–9) are missing.

E.159/61   15–16 Edward I   (1287–8)

No. 29 (m.1d), Mich.:
Allowance to Peter de la Mare, constable of Bristol, for money spent on sending building materials to Carmarthen and other supplies sent to Welsh castles: also allowances for expenses on Llywelyn, son of Dafydd ap Gruffydd, and Owain his brother kept in the castle.

No. 30 (m.3d), Hil.:
Allowance to be given to the sheriff of Yorkshire for money paid to Robert Tibetot, justice of West Wales, for building operations in castles in Wales.

No. 31 (m.9d), Pascha:
Richard Cam rendered such good service to the king against Rhys ap Maredudd that he is quit of his debt to the Exchequer.

No. 32 (m.10), Trin.:
Grants of privileges to the burgesses of Caernarvon.

No. 33, *ibid*:
In reply to a petition by Bernard de Auker, burgess of Caernarvon, the king grants him special protection. *C.P.R., 1281–92*, p. 192.

E.159/62   16–17 Edward I   (1288–9)

No. 34 (m.1), Mich.:
Allowance to the sheriff of Salop and Staffs for his expenses on Rhys ap Maelgwn and Cynan ap Maredudd, imprisoned in Bridgnorth castle. Introduction, p. xvii, n. 10.

No. 35 (m.10), Trin.:
The abbot of Sherborne paid 40m. into the chamber at Rhuddlan and is quit of his scutage for Wales.

No. 36 (m.10d), Trin.:
Writ of allowance of 22 May 1287 on behalf of Philip Willoughby, Gregory Rokesle and Ralph Dacre, collectors of the Thirtieth. Their payments included 200m. paid to Otto de Grandison and the Riccardi for building operations in Wales.

E.368/61   17–18 Edward I   (1289–90)

No. 37 (m.14), Pascha:
The Exchequer is to audit the account of Robert Tibetot, justice of West Wales, for the money he had spent on the building operations at Llanbadarn castle. Enr. Acc., E.372/134, m.2.

No. 38 (m.16), Trin.:
Allowance to Robert Tibetot, justice of Wales and constable of Nottingham castle, for Gruffydd ap Maredudd, a Welsh prisoner, kept there from 29 September 1283 until 26 May 1290.

E.159/63   17–18 Edward I   (1289–90)

No. 39 (m.8), Hil.:
Allowance to Bogo de Knovill', constable of Montgomery, for his expenses on the castle.

E.368/62   18–19 Edward I   (1290–1)

No. 40 (m.10d), Mich.:
Allowance to be made to the executors of William Perton, constable of Flint, of £19 of the 250m. owed by him which he had received from Llywelyn ap Gruffydd, then prince of Wales, at the end of Michaelmas 1280, in part payment of 500m. which the prince was accustomed to render to the king for Anglesey. Allowance is also made of 100s. being the annual fee paid to Tudor fil' 'Arewet' and David fil' Einion of the cantref of Englefield at 50s. each year for 1279–80. Allowance is also made for 50s. paid to the monks of Basingwerk for holding services in Flint castle for their robes and a stipend (1280). Cf. no. 26.

No. 40a, *ibid*:
Allowance to his executors of a further 300m. which he paid by the order of the king to William Sitones, constable of Rhuddlan. (E.159/64, m.8d, Hil.) Cf. no. 26.

No. 41 (m.32), Mich.:
Writ to the sheriff of Salop and Staffs to distrain the following marcher lords for reliefs: Stephen Summerner, Robert Chedles, Hamo fil' Ingeram le Marshal, William Butler of Wemme, Robert Beneret, Wilfred Bromhull, William fil' William Beneret, Edmund Mortimer son and heir of Roger Mortimer, Owen fil' Gruffydd. Cf. E.368/65, m.88, Mich.

No. 42 (m.34), Hil.:
Bogo de Knovill', late constable of Montgomery, is to be distrained for the arrears of the farm of Montgomery. Cf. no. 70.

E.159/64   18–19 Edward I   (1290–1)

No. 43 (m.3d), Mich.:
Warrant for the division of the earldom of Pembroke among the heirs.

No. 44 (m.28), Pascha:
A day for account is given to Robert de Belvoir, chamberlain of Snowdon, and Adam Wetenhale, chancellor of Wales and controller, to account at Michaelmas. They fail to account and are given another day 'quia Barones super compotum de Garderoba impediti fuerunt'. Cf. nos. 46, 48.

E.368/63   19–20 Edward I   (1291–2)

No. 45 (m.4), Mich.:
Ralph Broughton, in charge of the works at Llanbadarn castle, is quit in his account as he has accounted for £120 with which he was charged by special auditors and his account is kept in the Wardrobe, as the former keeper of the Wardrobe has testified. (E.159/65, m.6d, Mich.) Cf. no. 20.

No. 46 (m.5), *ibid*:
Allowance ordered in his account to Robert de Belvoir, chamberlain of Caernarvon, for money paid to Adam Wetenhale, chancellor of Wales and controller of Belvoir, for building operations there. (E.159/65, m.7, Mich.) Cf. nos. 44, 48.

No. 47 (m.10), Hil.:
Nicholas Brikeborn, viewer of building operations in Montgomery castle, claimed allowance of £53 7s. 9d. for the repair of houses in the castle by Bogo de Knovill'. (E.159/65, mm.12d, 16d, Hil.)

No. 48 (m.10d), Hil.:
Audit: Robert de Belvoir, chamberlain of (North) Wales, 2 February to 29 September 1291.
Sum due: £156 8s. 2¼d.
After allowances owes £64 14s. 10¾d., paid in 1292.
Enr. Acc. in *B.B.C.S* 14 (1952), p. 303.

Ibid, m.11:
Three letters of allowance for Robert de Belvoir, for payments made 29 September 1285 to 29 September 1291. (E.159/65, mm.13d, 14, Hil.)
Allowed in Enr. Acc., *B.B.C.S.* 14 (1951–2), pp. 240–1, 302–8. Cf. nos. 44, 46.

No. 49 (m.15), Pascha:
Allowances to Richard Abingdon, chamberlain of Caernarvon. (End torn off.) Contd. m.15d, second allocate 'per billam de Garderoba'. Enr. Acc. in *B.B.C.S.* 14 (1951), pp. 236–40.

E.159/65   19–20 Edward I   (1291–2)

No. 50 (m.8), Mich.:
Allowance to be made to the justice of Chester and constable of Rhuddlan for sums spent provisioning the castle.

No. 51, *ibid*:
Robert Tibetot, justice of Wales, is ordered to return to the merchants, who owned them, the goods he had recovered from Welshmen who had stolen them off the Isle of Sully (Glam).

No. 52 (m.12d), Hil.:
Allowance made to Walter Cambion, constable of Bamborough castle, for the expense of keeping Rhys ap Maelgwn and Cynan ap Maredudd. Introduction, p. xvii, n. 11.

No. 53 (m.28d), Recogn., Mich.:
Thomas Bray of Smoleshoe has made a recognizance of debt of 9m. to Retheric ap Gruffydd.

E.368/64   20–21 Edward I   (1292–3)

No. 54 (m.20), Pascha:
Audit: Robert de Belvoir, chamberlain of North Wales, 29 September 1291 to 29 March 1293, and for the arrears of the previous accounts (1285–91).
Sum due: £990 6s. 5¼d.
After allowances owes £269 6s. 5¼d. to be levied from his lands and benefices (E.159/66, m.26d, less complete). Enr. Acc. in *B.B.C.S.* 14 (1952), pp. 309—11. Part of chamberlain's roll for 1291–2 in *B.B.C.S.* 9 (1937), pp. 51–60.

No. 55 (m.26), Trin.:
Grant to William Clement, of the commote of Pennardd in Cardiganshire. (E.159/66, m.28d, Trin.). He is later made quit of rent for good service in the war (E.159/67, m.2, Mich.).

No. 56 (m.33), *ibid*:
Writ to Adam Wetenhale, chancellor of Wales and controller, to make allowances in the account of Robert de Belvoir, chamberlain, of payments made to William de Cykoun (Ciconiis), keeper of Conway castle.

No. 57 (m.64), Hil.:
The custodian of the spiritualities of the diocese of Llandaff during the vacancy has come to the Exchequer to satisfy the king for his arrears.

No. 58 (mm.65d, 66d), Pascha:
The temporalities of the bishopric of St. David's are to be held by Ralph Broughton during the vacancy. Enr. Acc., E.372/139, m.3d [vacancy 22 April to 11 October 1293].

E.159/66   20–21 Edward I   (1292–3)

No. 59 (mm.8–11d), Mich.:
Agreement after the death of William (V) de Braose (*d.* 1290), between his heir William (VI) and his widow Mary together with her son Richard. Mary owes to the king £227 15s. 10¼d. which William agreed to raise. Proceedings include (m.11d) a record of the debts due to William (V) in Wales and his goods there, totalling £416 13s. 9½d. It was agreed that the arrears of 800m. of a fine made by his Welsh tenants to William (V) should be levied from these tenants by William (VI) who requested a writ of aid under the Exchequer seal (mandate of 17 November 1292, m.8d).

Ibid (mm.42, 42d), Trin.:
William (VI) de Braose on 30 September 1293 denied at the Exchequer that Exchequer writs have ever been answered from Welsh marcher lordships and maintains that he does not owe a return to the demand to levy 800m. of a fine of his Welsh tenants (above, m.8d). It was replied for the Exchequer that Braose originally himself requested such a writ. After proceedings had been adjourned, Braose produced a letter of protection, on the king's service in Gascony, of 20 June 1294. Thereafter proceedings continued inconclusively until 30 Edward I (1301–2). (E.368/64, mm.9d, 10, a partial copy.)

E.368/65   21–22 Edward I   (1293–4)

No. 60 (m.1), Mich.:
Committal of the county of Merioneth and the castle and liberty of Bere to Robert FitzWalter for an annual rent of £300 6s. 8d.

No. 61, *ibid*:
Committal of Harlech castle to Robert Sandon.

No. 62 (m.17), Mich.:
Writ to the justice of Wales, enquiring by what terms John Giffard holds Is Cennen, with long endorsement (fuller on K.R. roll, E.159/67, m.9, Mich.). Cf. no. 65.

No. 63 (m.18), Mich.:
Allowance to the constable of Bamborough for the expenses of Rhys ap Maelgwn and Cynan ap Maredudd. Introduction, p. xvii, n. 11. (E.159/67, m.13, Mich.)

No. 64, *ibid*:
Allowance made in his account to the sheriff of Anglesey for his expenses at Dryslwyn against Rhys ap Maredudd. (E.159/67, m.13, Mich.)

E.159/67 21–22 Edward I (1293–4)

No. 65 (m.9), Mich.:
Royal enquiry addressed to Robert de Tibetot, justice of West Wales, whether anyone holding of John Giffard in his liberty in the commote of Is Cennen or any tenant of anybody else who holds by barony of the king in the county of Carmarthen is liable to the jurisdiction of the county court of Carmarthen for offences committed outside the liberty of which he is tenant. The jury said that such tenants come under the jurisdiction of the county court. They adduced ten cases from the past. These included the case of a certain son of one Magnel, tenant of Maredudd ap Rhys of the commote of Catheiniog, who had broken into the barony of Guy Brian of Laugharne, and was, later, on his return into the liberty of Maredudd, imprisoned by Maredudd. The English county court of Carmarthen took cognizance of the offence and the offender, as a Welshman, was transferred to the Welsh county court, by the judgement of which he was hanged. Both Maredudd and Guy had previously sued jurisdiction over the case for their respective courts, but this was denied to them. *C.P.R.*, *1292–1301*, p. 56. Cf. no. 62.

No. 66 (m.53), Trin.:
The tenants of John de Warenne in Wales are prepared to pay their part of the Tenth to Reginald Grey, justice of Chester, who is charged to receive it.

No. 67 (m.58), Trin.:
Bishop Thomas (Bek) of St. David's owed at his death a debt to the Riccardi of Lucca. His executors assign to the Riccardi a part of the debts due by various people to the deceased bishop in part repayment.

No. 68 (mm.63, 63d), Trin.:
Edmund Mortimer is attached to answer the king for alleged resistance to the collectors of the Fifteenth (granted in 1291) who intended to levy the tax in his lands in the county of Shropshire, preventing them through his bailiffs and other officials from doing this. It is alleged that it was his purpose to remove these lands from the county and to add them to his liberty outside the county. Mortimer denied the accusation, maintaining that in his lands within the county, except at Wigmore, he allowed the levy to proceed and that he had always recognised the jurisdiction of the king's itinerant justices over his tenants there. At Wigmore his tenants do not answer the summons of the itinerant justices and the king's writ does not run there and the jurisdiction belongs solely to the lord of the liberty and has done so from time immemorial. The tenants there are free from the royal taxes and the king, slightly more than a year after the concession of the Fifteenth, requested from Mortimer, as from other lords of Wales,

a special concession of a Fifteenth of the goods of tenants inside the afore-said liberty (of Wigmore). The king appointed a special collector for the same and the tenants fully satisfied him (levy of 1293). Before Mortimer had conceded this grant the ordinary Shropshire collectors had wanted to collect the Fifteenth inside the liberty and were challenged by Mortimer's bailiff, Hugh Picard, to show by what warrant they were acting thus, whereupon they desisted from further collecting the tax. Mortimer denied that he had otherwise impeded the collectors anywhere, but they continued to insist that he had impeded them.

E.368/66   22–23 Edward I   (1294–5)

No. 69 (m.43), Pascha:
Instructions concerning the seizure of carts for taking the royal treasury (of the household) into Wales.

E.159/68   22–23 Edward I   (1294–5)

No. 70 (m.6), Hil.:
Bogo de Knovill', constable of Montgomery, is pardoned the arrears of his farm. C.Cl.R., 1288–96, p. 105 (1290). Cf. no. 42.

No. 71 (m.68), Special membrane:
A schedule of prelates who on 30 September 1294, in the first concession of the clerical Moiety, promised to make lump payments. Includes the bishops of St. Asaph (£40) and Bangor (£40).

No. 72 (m.71), ibid:
Writs to the collectors of the Moiety in Wales to send the money which they have collected as quickly as possible.

E.368/67   23–24 Edward I   (1295–6)

No. 73 (m.4), Advent. Vic., Mich.:
The sheriff of Hampshire came and brought writs of allowance of £26 1s. for expenses on various unnamed Welsh prisoners.

No. 74 (m.5), Comm., Mich.:
The keepers are to put Beaumaris and Caernarvon in a better state of defence. (E.159/69, m.38.) B.B.C.S. 15 (1952), pp. 62–6.

No. 75 (m.10), Brevia pro Rege, Mich.:
Instructions for corn to be sent from Ireland to Wales.

No. 76, ibid:
Order to Hugh Leominster, chamberlain of North Wales, to purchase provisions (enumerated) for Welsh castles.

No. 77, *ibid*:
Instructions to the constable of Bristol to send supplies to Caernarvon and other castles.

No. 78 (m.10d), *ibid*:
The constable of St. Briavels castle (Glos) is to deliver munitions to the constable of Bristol who is to send them to Wales.

No. 79 (m.14), Fines, Mich.:
View of the account of Adam Weston for the time when he was custodian of the lands of Dafydd ap Gruffydd in England. (Allowances, E.159/69, m.8d, Br. d. Bar., Mich.; Writ, *ibid*, m.23, Br. d. Bar., Hil.; View, m.30, Manuc.)

No. 80 (m.53d), Recogn., Trin.:
The sheriff of Norfolk is to send the ship which he provisioned for the king's service at Caernarvon to Gascony with corn.

No. 80a (m.69), Prec. super Comp., Mich.:
Welsh hostages (Salop and Staffs). Introduction, p. xviii, n. 23.

No. 80b (m.70), *ibid*:
Welsh hostages (Northampton). Introduction, p. xix, n. 31.

No. 81 (m.70d), *ibid*, Pascha:
Welsh hostages (Hereford). Introduction, p. xviii, n. 24. (E.159/69, m.56.)

No. 81a, *ibid*:
Welsh hostages (Hereford). Introduction, p. xviii, n. 24.

No. 81b (m.71), *ibid*:
Welsh hostages (Wilts). Introduction, p. xix, n. 33.

No. 81c (m.72), *ibid*, Trin.:
Welsh hostages (Notts and Derby). Introduction, p. xix, n. 29.

No. 82 (m.72d), *ibid*, Trin.:
Welsh hostages (Surrey and Sussex). Introduction, p. xviii, n. 27. (E.159/69, m.57d.)

No. 83 (m.73), *ibid*:
Welsh hostages (Yorkshire). Introduction, p. xix, n. 29.

No. 84 (m.73d), *ibid*:
Welsh hostages (Somerset and Dorset). Introduction, p. xix, n. 32. (E.159/69, m.58d.)

E.159/69   23–24 Edward I   (1295–6)

No. 85 (m.4), Br. d. Bar., Mich: Privy Seal, Hengham, 29 September 1295:
Instructions to the Exchequer to write to James of St. George and Walter
Hereford, custodians of building operations, about the defences of
Caernarvon and Beaumaris castles. The letter is *infra*, m.38, and is printed
in *B.B.C.S.* XV (1952), p. 62. Later proceedings occur on ms. 24, 25, and
are printed, *ibid*, pp. 63–5.

No. 86 (m.8), *ibid*:
Welsh hostages (Oxon and Berks). Introduction, p. xix, n. 31.

No. 87 (m.54), Prec. super Comp., Mich.:
Allowance to the sheriff of Salop and Staffs, including money paid to
various Welshmen for service, money for the transport of 30 Welsh
rebels to England, and the expenses of workmen sent from Staffs to
Caernarvon. Introduction, p. xviii, n. 23.

No. 87a (m.54d), *ibid*:
Welsh hostages (Lincoln). Introduction, p. xix, n. 30.

No. 88 (m.55), *ibid*:
Welsh hostages (Northampton). Introduction, p. xix, n. 31.

No. 89 (m.55d), *ibid*:
Welsh hostages (Warwick and Leicester). Introduction, p. xix, n. 31.

No. 90 (m.56), *ibid*, Pascha:
Welsh hostages (Wilts). Introduction, p. xix, n. 33.

No. 90a (m.57), *ibid*, Trin.:
Welsh hostages (Notts and Derby). Introduction, p. xix, n. 29.

No. 90b, *ibid*:
Audit of the account of Henry, bishop of St. David's collector of the clerical
Tenth in his diocese. Owes £250 16s. Allowances for a sum paid to John
Mansel, king's clerk. Owes £160 11s. 8d. Later on declared quit.

E.368/68   24–25 Edward I   (1296–7)

No. 91 (m.5), Communia, Trin.:
Hugh Leominster, chamberlain of North Wales and custodian of the lands
of Queen Eleanor there, is to reply for the issues of her lands.

No. 92, *ibid*:
Thomas Macclesfield is similarly to reply for her lands in Chester and Flint·
(E.159/70, m.67d.)

No. 93 (m.8d), Communia, Mich.: York, 22 February 1296:
Welsh hostages (Salop and Staffs). (E.159/70, mm.4d, 80.) Introduction, p. xviii, n. 23.

No. 94 (m.25), Communia, Hil.:
Memorandum that Adam Wetenhale, former controller of North Wales at the time of Robert de Belvoir, could not produce his rolls. He said that two years before, when the Welsh rose against the king in Snowdonia, they destroyed the goods and chattels of himself and all the English, and all the rolls and memoranda pertaining to his office were burnt by them. (E.159/70, m.60d.)

No. 95 (m.26), *ibid*:
Order to distrain Robert de Belvoir, chamberlain of North Wales, for the arrears of £269 6s. 5¼d. of the issues of his office. Cf. no. 166.

No. 96 (m.41), *ibid*, Pascha:
Audit of the account of the constable of Bristol including claims by him for the expenses of Owen, son of Dafydd ap Gruffydd, for other Welsh prisoners, and for sums spent for munitions sent to Wales. (E.159/70, m.97.) Introduction, p. xvii, n. 8.

No. 98 (m.47), *ibid*, Trin.:
Audit of the account of the constable of St. Briavel's, Gloucestershire, including claims for the expenses of Welsh hostages and the expenses of sending arms to Wales. (E.159/70, m.86, Hil.) Introduction, p. xviii, n. 25.

No. 99 (m.48), *ibid*:
Welsh hostages (York). Introduction, p. xix, n. 29. (E.159/70, mm.28, 85, 85d.)

No. 100, *ibid*:
Allowance to Bogo de Knovill', constable of Montgomery, in his account for £40 which he should have received as the ransom of two Welsh hostages. (E.159/70, ms.11d, 28.)

No. 101 (m.51d), Communia, Trin.:
Memorandum that on 22 July 1297 it was agreed in the parliament at Westminster by the king and his council that demands for the scutages for the armies in Wales in 1277 and 1282 should be respited until the king should further ordain about them.

No. 102 (m.57), *ibid*:
Fine of 20s. to the king for confirming the land grant to the abbey of La Pulle (Welshpool), West Wales.

No. 103 (m.73), Prec. super Comp., Mich.:
Welsh hostages (Wilts). Introduction, p. xix, n. 33. (E.159/70, m.80.)

No. 104 (m.74), *ibid*:
Welsh hostages (Hants). Introduction, *ibid*.

No. 105 (m.74d), *ibid*:
Welsh hostages (Northumberland). Introduction, p. xix, n. 29. (E.159/70, m.81.)

No. 106 (m.75), *ibid*:
Welsh hostages (Oxon and Berks). Introduction, p. xix, n. 31. (E.159/70, m.81d.)

No. 107 (m.75d), *ibid*:
Welsh hostages (Hereford). Introduction, p. xviii, n. 24. (E.159/70, m.87, Hil.)

No. 108 (m.77d), *ibid*:
Welsh hostages (Lincs). Introduction, p. xix, n. 30. (E.159/70, m.87, Hil.)

No. 109 (m.78), *ibid*:
Welsh hostages (Cumberland and Westmorland). Introduction, p. xix, n. 29.

No. 109a, *ibid*:
Welsh hostages (Notts and Derby). Introduction, p. xix, n. 29.

No. 109b (m.78d), *ibid*, Pascha:
Welsh hostages (York). Introduction, p. xix, n. 29.

No. 110 (mm.79, 79d), *ibid*:
Welsh hostages (Gloucester). Introduction, p. xviii, n. 25. (E.159/70, m.37d.)

E.159/70   24–25 Edward I   (1296–7)

No. 111 (m.4), Mich.:
Concerning a petition by the prior of Llanthony.

No. 112 (mm.25d, 30, 85), Pascha:
Welsh hostages (Notts and Derby). Introduction, p. xix, n. 29.

No. 113 (m.37), Trin.:
Allowance in his account to John Giffard, constable of Builth, for his expenses in repairing the castle there after the recent rebellion in Wales.

No. 114 (m.81d), Mich.:
Welsh hostages (Northampton). Introduction, p. xix, n. 31.

No. 115 (m.97d):
Writs to the sheriff of Pembrokeshire and the bailiffs of Haverfordwest and Carmarthen to distrain Thomas de Rupe, sheriff of Yorkshire, who has lands in their bailiwicks.

E.368/69 25–26 Edward I (1297–8)

No. 116 (mm.5d, 12), Comm., Trin.:
Writ of enquiry into the goods of the late Hugh Cressingham, including Welsh ones in Carmarthen, Cardigan and Haverfordwest.

No. 117 (m.19d), Br. Irr., Mich.:
Welsh hostages (Oxon and Berks). Introduction, p. xix, n. 31.

No. 118 (m.25), *ibid*:
Two writs concerning the movement and payment of troops from North Wales. (E.159/71, mm.105, 109d.)

No. 119 (m.25d), *ibid*:
Hugh Leominster, chamberlain of North Wales, is promised allowance for money spent by him out of the issues of the lands of Queen Eleanor as he is short of money. Also *infra*, m.27d.

No. 120 (m.27d), *ibid*:
Order to the chamberlain of Dublin to pay money to the chamberlain of North Wales.

No. 121, *ibid*:
Order to the constable of Bristol to send arms to North Wales.

No. 122 (m.29), *ibid*:
Writ to the justice of Wales concerning the choice of foot soldiers to fight in Scotland.

No. 123 (m.30), *ibid*:
Writ concerning the expenses needed for 3,000 foot soldiers sent from London to Aberconway and thence to Newcastle on Tyne.

No. 124 (m.50), Communia, Hil.:
Writ in response to a petition concerning the illegal seizure of wool in Haverfordwest. (E.159/71, m.29.)

No. 125 (m.55d), *ibid*:
Welsh hostages (Hereford). Introduction, p. xviii, n. 24. (E.159/71, m.89.)

No. 126 (m.56d), *ibid*:
Welsh hostages (Northampton). Introduction, p. xix, n. 31.

No. 127 (m.60d), *ibid*:
Writ to Hugh Leominster concerning foodstuffs sent to Caernarvon.

No. 128, *ibid*:
Order to the bailiff of Portsmouth to send goods by ship to Caernarvon.
(E.159/71, m.112d.)

No. 129 (m.88), Recorda, Trin.:
Welsh hostages (Northumberland). Introduction, p. xix, n. 31.

No. 130 (m.88d), Communia, Trin.:
Welsh hostages (York). Introduction, p. xix, n. 29.
Welsh hostages (Northumberland). *Ibid.*

No. 131 (m.110), Br. Ret., Mich.:
Mandate to the justice of North Wales to distrain Odo de Nevet, hospitaller,
and Madog ap David of Hendwr.

No. 132 (m.121), Prec. super Comp., Trin.:
Sheriff of Gloucester requests allowance for expenses in connection with
the Welsh War.

E.159/71   25–26 Edward I   (1297–8)

No. 133 (m.5d), Comm., Mich.:
Detailed allowances made to the constable of Bristol for expenses connected
with the Welsh War, including £1,000 sent to William de Valence, earl of
Pembroke, captain of the army in Wales, and allowance for the expenses of
Welsh hostages in Bristol castle.

No. 134 (m.19d), Br. d. Bar., Hil.: Bury St. Edmunds, 15 November 1296:
Welsh hostages (Salop and Staffs). Introduction, p. xviii, n. 23.

No. 135 (m.33d), *ibid*, Pascha: St. Albans, 25 April 1298
Robert FitzWalter is excused the rent of Bere castle (Merioneth) because of
his service in Gascony. Cf. E.159/76, m.15, Br. d. Bar., Pascha.

No. 136 (m.37d), *ibid*: Privy Seal, Impeton, 5 May 1298:
Welsh burgesses who have had their wool unjustly seized and who have
petitioned the king are to have it returned.

No. 137 (m.50), *ibid*. Trin.: Castleacre, 8 February 1297:
Welsh hostages (York and Northumberland). Introduction, p. xviii, n. 23.

No. 138 (m.70), *ibid*:
Inquest into the goods of Hugh Cressingham including those in the counties
of Carmarthen and Cardigan and the bailiwick of Haverfordwest.

No. 139 (m.108d), Br. Irr., Mich.:
Writs concerning the castle works in Wales.

No. 140 (m.113d), *ibid*, Hil.:
Tax collectors in Salop are to deliver £50 for building operations on North Wales castles.

No. 141 (m.118), Br. Ret., Trin.:
Allowance to the steward of Haverford for his expenses in maintaining the prior of St. Clears (Pembs) whose goods have been confiscated as the head of an alien religious house.

Ibid:
The king wishes to know the annual income of the alien priory of St. Clears (Pembs).

E.368/70   26–27 Edward I   (1298–9)

No. 142 (m.34), Br. d. Bar., Pascha: Westminster, 28 March 1299:
Allowance to John Botetourt, constable of St. Briavels castle (Glos) for expenses caused by the recent invasion of the Welsh. (E.159/72, m.24.)

No. 143 (m.39d), *ibid*: Stepney, 16 May 1298:
The barons of the Exchequer are to provide remedy for certain (unnamed) petitions of the Welsh, presented at Stepney.

Ibid: Stepney, 13 May 1298:
There follows a petition by the burgesses of Cardigan into the allegedly illegal taking of their wool.

No. 144 (m.65), Br. Irr., Pascha:
Mandate to Hugh Leominster, custodian of the lands of the deceased Queen Eleanor in Snowdon and Anglesey, to supersede until the next parliament certain demands for payment in the commote of Menai according to the petitions presented by the tenants thereof. It recites the petitions of 'Gronici Cragh' of Trefgarnect (Tregarnedd), tenant of the manor of Roffeyr, David ap Howel and Howel ap 'Conewrik', Welshmen, which include the following complaints:
1.   Although Goronwy ought to hold the bailiwick of the commote of Menai free of charge, and this had been confirmed by an inquisition before Robert Standon, justice of Wales, twenty shillings have been illegally exacted from him each year.
2.   The demesne of the manor had been leased for seven years to the said tenants at the yearly rent of £20 6s. 8d. by the late Queen Eleanor. Because of the poverty of the tenants the annual rent of the last two years of the lease was reduced by her by ten marks a year; (after her death) the annual rent in 22 and 23 Edward I amounted to £12 and thereafter to £10. But Leominster has been demanding £22 a year for the entire period of his custody.

3.   Two other individual complaints.
Letter under Exchequer seal of 26 May 1299 by warrant of a mandate of
Great Seal and two petitions transmitted to the Exchequer.

No. 145, *ibid*:
William Pedirton, justice of Wales, is notified that Gruffydd ap Rhys holds
the township of 'Cumlek' in South Wales of royal gift and is not to be
distrained for rent.

No. 146 (m.65d), *ibid*, Trin.:
The chamberlain of Wales is to see to the provisioning of various North
Wales castles.

No. 147 (m.91), St. et Vis., Trin.:
The account of the justice of Chester includes his expenses for the payment
of Welsh troops and for works on Welsh castles. (E.159/72, mm.88, 88d.)
(E.368/71, mm.12, 12d.)

E.159/72   26–27 Edward I   (1298–9)
No. 148 (mm.40, 40d), Br. d. Bar., Mich.: Jedburgh, 7 October 1298:
Welsh hostages (Surrey and Sussex).

No. 149 (m.54), Comm., Hil.:
Order for the sale of goods of the late Humphrey de Bohun, earl of Hereford
(including Welsh ones).

No. 150 (m.83), Prec. super Comp., Hil.:
Welsh hostages (Hereford). Introduction, p. xviii, n. 24.

No. 151 (m.90d), *ibid*, Trin.:
Welsh hostages (Norfolk and Suffolk).

E.368/71   27–28 Edward I   (1299–1300)

No. 152 (m.18d), Recorda, Mich.:
Adam Wetenhale, chancellor of Wales, is to come to the Exchequer to
certify to the barons about various expenses of Robert de Belvoir,
chamberlain. (E.159/73, m.24d.)

No. 153, *ibid*:
Summons to account to Patrick Haselwell, collector of the Fifteenth in
Flint.

No. 154 (m.24), D.d., Mich.:
A day for account is given to Thomas Macclesfield, custodian of the lands
of Queen Eleanor, including those of Hope and Overton in Flintshire,
North Wales. (E.159/73, m.53d.)

No. 155 (m.27), Br. d. Bar., Hil.: Wetherby, 13 January 1300:
Welsh hostages (Hereford). Introduction, p. xviii, n. 24.

No. 156 (m.27d), *ibid*: Durham, 4 December 1299:
Detailed writ of allowance to Robert de Belvoir, chamberlain of North
Wales.

No. 157 (m.29), *ibid*:
Writ to John Havering, justice of Wales, to array 2,000 foot soldiers for
the war in Scotland. Cf. no. 165.

No. 158 (m.43d), Br. d. Bar., Trin.: Westminster, 14 May 1300:
Grant to the burgesses of Overton (Flint).

No. 159 (m.54d), Br. Irr., Hil.:
Hugh Leominster, chamberlain of North Wales, is ordered to come to the
parliament at York and leave provisions sufficient for one year in the
Welsh castles.

No. 160 (m.56), *ibid*, Trin.:
Writ directing the escheator of Chester to pay the arrears of his annual fee
to Rotheric fil' Griffin. (Allowance for payment, E.368/72, m.51, Br. Irr.,
Mich.)

No. 161, *ibid*:
Bogo de Knovill' is to make necessary repairs to Montgomery castle. Also
infra, m. 65d. (E.159/73, m.61, Br. Irr., Trin.)

No. 162 (m.61), Br. Ret., Mich.:
Walter Hakelut, custodian of Haverfordwest, is to distrain John Cokay
and Richard Parmenter, customs collectors, for £150 2s. 4d. which they
owe for wool sold to them by the king.

No. 163 (m.64d), *ibid*, Trin.:
The justice of Wales is to distrain Tudor ap Karnet and Blethyn Vychan to
render account for the Fifteenth conceded in the cantrefs of Rhos and
Rhufoniog in the lands of Henry de Lacy, earl of Lincoln.

No. 164 (m.65d), *ibid*:
The justice of Wales is to go and supervise the provisioning of the West
Wales castles of which Robert Tibetot was constable until his death.

No. 165 (mm.66d, 67), *ibid*:
Richard Havering is sent to Wales to collect £2,000 for the king's use,
needed for the payment of foot soldiers to be sent to York and to Scotland
Cf. no. 157.

No. 166 (m.69), St. et Vis., Mich.:

Audit: Robert de Belvoir, chamberlain of North Wales, 29 March 1293 to 29 September 1294.

Sum due: £2,019 0s. 7d., as in Enrolled Account, *B.B.C.S.* 14 (1952), p. 312, including arrears of previous accounts.

After allowances owes £196 18s. 3d., but £150 are to be charged to other persons. He successfully petitioned for the restoration of his lands and goods, previously in the king's hands, for the arrears of previous accounts. Cf. no. 95.

Arrears and demand for account for 29 September 1294 to 10 July 1295, when he was replaced as chamberlain, are charged E.372/153, Adhuc Res. Notts and Derby, but no results of further accounting are recorded there.

No. 167 (m.70), *ibid*:

Audit of the account of Patrick Haselwell and James de la Pulle, taxers and collectors of the Fifteenth conceded in the county of Flint in Wales, 1292. They owe £118 10s. 1¾d., and they said that other than that they could not levy and did not levy. They levied a part and then the war broke out on the morrow of Michaelmas and they could not levy even a quarter of the Fifteenth and dared not. After this time they levied nothing because many of those assessed were killed and others had very little left. Introduction, p. xxi.

No. 168 (mm.71d, 73d), *ibid*, Pascha:

View of the account of the bailiff of St. Briavels (Glos) including his Welsh expenses. (E.159/73, m.77d.)

No. 169 (m.74d), Prec. super Comp., Mich.:

Welsh hostages (Northumberland). Introduction, p. xix, n. 29. (E.159/73, mm.9d, 10, 65d.)

E.159/73   27–28 Edward I   (1299–1300)

No. 170 (m.16), Br. d. Bar., Pascha: Stamford, 30 April 1300, warranted by bill of exchequer:

Welsh hostages (Notts.). Introduction, p. xix, n. 29.

No. 171 (m.19), *ibid*, Trin.: Flint, 13 September 1298 and Windsor, 27 July 1299:

Two writs of allowance to Roger Lestrange, bailiff of Dinas Bran and Oswestry, for foot soldiers sent to Rhuddlan.

No. 172, *ibid*: Westminster, 20 March 1300:

Demand to the justice of Chester for the payment of his arrears from the farm of the cantref of Englefield and for the goods in Flint and Rhuddlan.

No. 173 (m.57), D.d., Trin.:

John Godele, assigned to go to Wales for money conceded by the Welsh, is to come to York as quickly as possible. Introduction, p. xxi.

E.368/72   28–29 Edward I   (1300–1)

No. 174 (m.38d), D.d., Pascha:
A day for account is given to William Birkhill and Robert Standon to render account as sheriffs of Merioneth and Richard Pyncles as sheriff of Caernarvon respectively.

No. 175, *ibid*:
A day for account is given to Hugh Leominster, chamberlain of North Wales.

No. 177 (m.39), Br. d. Bar., Trin.: Privy Seal, Abbey of St. Thomas iuxta
  Stafford, 20 May 1301:
Writ of the prince of Wales to the Exchequer. Respite in rendering account to be allowed to Walter Hakelut, justice of South Wales, as he is collecting foot soldiers for Scotland there. (E.159/74, m.22.)

No. 178 (m.41), *ibid*: Leeds, 3 July 1305:
Similar respite, at the request of the prince of Wales, allowed to Hugh Leominster, chamberlain of North Wales.

No. 179 (no membrane number, as the bottom of the roll has disintegrated),
  St. et Vis., Mich.:
Debt of John Havering, justice of Wales, including that resulting from his expenses on Welsh castles.

No. 180, *ibid*:
Audit of the account of the constable of Bristol including his expenses on Welsh prisoners. Cf. Introduction, p. xviii, n. 27. (E.159/74, m.64d.)

No. 181, *ibid*, Pascha:
Welsh hostages (Warwick and Leicester). Introduction, p. xix, n. 31.

E.159/74   28–29 Edward I   (1300–1)

No. 182 (m.7d), Br. d. Bar., Hil.: Lincoln, 26 February 1301:
Allowance to be made to John Havering, justice of Wales, for the arrears of his fee when he renders account.

No. 183 (m.65), *ibid*, Pascha:
Welsh hostages (Northumberland). Cf. Introduction, p. xix, n. 29.

No. 184 (m.66), *ibid*:
Audit of the account of the escheator of Chester, including payments made to the chamberlain of North Wales.

The L.T.R. roll for 29–30 Edward I (1301–2) is missing.

E.159/75   29–30 Edward I   (1301–2)

No. 185 (m.7d), Br. d. Bar., Mich.: Dunipace, 16 October 1301:
The barons are to make allowance to Hugh Leominster for his expenses on building operations on Caernarvon castle.

No. 186 (m.17), *ibid*, Pascha: Devizes, 28 April 1302:
The king wishes to ascertain the value of the lands in Wales of the late Richard, earl of Arundel. Also *infra*, m.41d, Communia, Pascha. Order for extents of the lands to be made.

No. 187 (m.20), *ibid*, Trin.: Chartham, 13 June 1302:
The king wants to know the annual value of the lands of the prince of Wales so that debts to him can be exacted.

No. 188 (m.34), Recorda, Pascha:
Yerewardus fil' Yerewardi de Riston, attached to reply for a relief, says he holds his lands of Montgomery castle in the possession of the prince of Wales, has paid relief to him and is quit.

No. 189 (m.35d), *ibid*:
Writs concerning the provisioning of South Wales castles by the prior of Carmarthen.

No. 190 (m.54d), D.d., Mich.:
A day is given for William of Cardiff to answer for the relief owed as heir of Paulyn of Cardiff.

No. 191 (m.66) (special membrane):
Assignment of £4,000 from the Fifteenth to be levied in the Marches to Welsh foot soldiers as their pay for service in Scotland. Also *infra*, m.79 (two writs). Cf. no. 202.

No. 192 (m.84), Prec. super Comp., Mich.:
Welsh hostages (Northumberland). Introduction, p. xix, n. 29.

No. 193 (m.87d), *ibid*, Pascha:
Welsh hostages (Hereford). Introduction, p. xviii, n. 24.

E.368/73   30–31 Edward I   (1302–3)

No. 194 (m.16d), Recorda, Mich.:
List of arrears of rent of tenants in Irchingeld (Archenfield):

Roger Kari	32s.	6d.
Adam ap Wrennon	4s.	2d.
Adam ap Llywelyn	3s.	6d.

'Seyntmariebirches'	Adam ap Robert	2s.	2d.
	Hugo de Birches	3s.	4d.
'Markwyneston'	Seysel de eodem	2s.	6d.
	Seysel ap Adam	7s.	6d.
'Achelbogh'	Kneythe Goch	4s.	6d.
	Adam Suaunt	5s.	od.
'Langaran'	Yeuan ap Gurgenou'	10s.	
'Treredennok'	Gruffydd ap David	5s.	
'Kilreyk'	David Robba	2s.	6d.
	Kenwreyk Kathken	2s.	6d.
	Yeuan Schanka	2s.	6d.
	Gruffydd ap Madog	3s.	4d.
	Yeuan ap Wynlyn	1s.	8d.
	David Vaghan	2s.	6d.
'Kilren'	Craddock Suaunt	5s.	od.
'Treygosset'	Gwrenno ap Yeuan	5s.	od.
'Trewalch'	Seysel Walht	2s.	6d.
Llangennock	Meuryk ap Wrenno	15s.	2d.
Trebereth	Wrennon Trebereth	2s.	6d.
	Leukyn fil' Yeuan	21s.	6d.
'Trelesseni'	Walter Marmyon	2s.	6d.
'Trerrybil'	Simon ap Ithel	2s.	6d.
	Hynyd fil' Yereward	5s.	
'Treganan'	William ap Oweyn	3s.	4d.
'Treyenan'	Yeuan ap Adam	4s.	10d.
	Leuky fil' Seysel	2s.	6d.
Trelank	Gruffydd ap Ieuan	5s.	
	Yereward de Kilbrey	3s.	4d.
	Wassanfreyd ap Wrennou'	1s.	8d.
'Brenychyn'	Philip ap Eynon	10s.	
	Leukyn fil' Wogan	1s.	8d.
	Yeuan ap David	1s.	8d.
'Tresele'	Perwer fil' Wreno	5s.	
'Hendrewren'	Ieuan ap Wylyn	3s.	
Retyr	Richard le Bret	42s.	
Henthelau	Philip ap Adam	5s.	
Pengethly	Wrenno do eodem	3s.	6d.
	Nest de eodem	7s.	6d.
Davidston	Adam ap Maredudd	1s.	8d.
'Kynnadeston'	John de eodem	6s.	
	William ap Phelipe	2s.	4d.
Pencoyt	Adam ap Seysel	5s.	
	Philip fil. Johannis de eodem	5s.	
Leytheston	Maddog ap Johannes	2s.	6d.

(E.159/76, m.24d, Recorda.)

No. 195 (m.30d), *ibid*, Hil.:

Complaint by two burgesses of Conway that Master James of St. George, master of the works at Conway, had purveyed goods worth £108 18s. and

had not paid for them. Endorsed that they are to be reimbursed.
(E.159/76, m.8.)

No. 196 (m.43d), Fines, Pascha:
Edmund Mortimer is to reply for the relief due for his land of Radnor. He
appeals concerning the relief on the barony of Wigmore.

No. 197 (m.47), Br. d. Bar., Trin.: Westminster, 12 August 1302:
Adam fil' Adam Bernard, custodian of the manors of 'Boudon' and
'Haverbergh' (Leic) pleads that he has been charged with the rent for them
for a period when the king had granted them to Gruffydd ap Madog.
(E.159/76, m.17.)

No. 198 (m.47d), *ibid*: Perth, 28 June 1303:
Allowance to be made to Richard de Mascy, justice of Chester, for his
expenses on Flint and Rhuddlan castles. (E.159/76, m.18d.)

No. 199 (m.71), Br. Ret., Trin.:
Enquiry is to be made into what money the collectors of the Moiety in
South Wales have managed to collect.

No. 200 (mm.72, 72d), *ibid*, Mich.:
Welsh hostages (Chester). Introduction, p. xviii, n. 26.

No. 201 (m.79d), Prec. super Comp., Hil.:
Welsh hostages (Hereford). Introduction, p. xviii, n. 24.

E.159/76   30–31 Edward I   (1302–3)

No. 202 (m.6), Br. d. Bar., Hil.: Odiham, 8 January 1303:
The lands and goods of the collectors of the Fifteenth (in the Marches)
are to be taken into the king's hands unless they fulfil the assignment of the
tax to Welsh foot soldiers. Cf. no. 191. Also *infra*, m.71d. Brevia pro Rege,
Hil.: the sheriffs of Notts, Derby and Salop are to answer for their goods if
they fail to make the assignment. (E.368/74, m.19, Recorda, Mich.)

No. 203 (m.59), D.d., Mich.:
A day for account is given to the prior of Llanthony, collector of the clerical
subsidy in the diocese of St. David's. Cf. no. 206.

No. 204, *ibid*:
Ditto to the prior of Carmarthen for the collection of money from the
archdeaconries of Carmarthen and Cardiganshire. Cf. no. 206.

No. 205 (m.79d), St. et Vis., Pascha:
Welsh hostages (Norfolk and Suffolk). Cf. appendix 1.

E.368/74 31–32 Edward I (1303–4)

No. 206 (m.15), Recorda, Mich.:
The priors of Llanthony and Carmarthen are attached to render account for the clerical subsidy. Cf. nos. 203, 204.

No. 207 (m.19d), *ibid*:
The prior of Llanthony claimed that his predecessor had paid all that he owed as collector of the clerical subsidy in the archdeaconry of Brecon and the archdeaconry of St. David's in the diocese of St. David's, and that he had been unjustly distrained for £204 3s. 1d. by the sheriff of Hereford. (E.159/77, m.23, Recorda, Mich.) Cf. no. 217.

No. 208 (m.60d), Br. Ret., Mich.:
The sheriff of Notts and Derby is to distrain Owen son of Griffin fil' Gwenwynwyn, or his heir if he is dead.

No. 209 (m.68d), St. et Vis., Mich.:
Audit of the account of the collectors of the Fifteenth (Notts and Derby). They claimed to have delivered £228 2s. 11d. to Robert Drishill, clerk of Edward, prince of Wales, for the works of certain Welsh castles. (E.159/77, m.65d.)

E.159/77 31–32 Edward I (1303–4)

No. 210 (m.62), Br. Ret., Mich.:
The ecclesiastical Tenth, granted by Pope Boniface VIII, is to be collected even though the Pope is dead, and no frivolous excuses will be accepted (includes writs to Welsh collectors).

E.368/75 32–33 Edward I (1304–5)

No. 211 (m.8), Br. d. Bar., Mich.: Burstwick, 22 October 1304:
Welsh hostages (Norfolk). Sons of Rhys ap Maredudd.

No. 212 (m.39d), *ibid*, Pascha: Westminster, 1 April 1305:
Roger Mortimer is pardoned a debt of £120 which he had received from the Wardrobe for the expense of taking soldiers to Dryslwyn.

No. 213 (m.57), Recorda, Trin.:
Richard Havering, collector of the Welsh subsidy granted for the Scottish war (1300), sought allowance of £13 7s. 2½d. which he had paid to Ednyfed, master of the Hospital [of St. John] in North Wales. Cf. introduction, p. xxxi.

No. 214 (mm.85, 86), Prec. super Comp., Mich.:
Welsh hostages (Hereford and Norfolk). Cf. introduction, p. xviii, n. 24.

E.159/78   32–33 Edward I   (1304–5)

No. 215 (m.70d), St. et Vis., Hil.:
Audit of the account of the sheriff of Salop and Staffs, including money raised from the lands of the prince of Wales in Montgomeryshire.

E.368/76   33–34 Edward I   (1305–6)

No. 216 (m.15), Recorda, Mich.:
Memorandum: The Exchequer had demanded £1,000 from Robert de Belvoir, chamberlain, and Adam Wetenhale, controller of North Wales, which they had received from William Louth, keeper of the Wardrobe. Wetenhale then claimed that this £1,000 was in fact received from the Lucchese merchants and that Belvoir had fully accounted for the money. The barons are to examine the rolls. They maintain that the first £1,000 are the ones for which Belvoir and Wetenhale had accounted in 1288, but that they received the other money, still charged to them, in 1289 and must still account for it. (E.159/79, m.24d.)

No. 217 (m.75d), Br. Ret., Pascha:
The sheriff of Herefordshire is to exact £111 12s. 9¾d. owed by the prior of Llanthony, collector of the clerical subsidy in the archdeaconry of Brecon and the diocese of St. David's. Cf. no. 207.

No. 218 (m.84d), Prec. super Comp., Hil.:
Welsh hostages (Norfolk and Suffolk).

E.159/79   33–34 Edward I   (1305–6)

No. 219 (m.5d), Br. d. Bar., Mich.: Bolkestede, 27 June 1305:
Welsh hostages (Windsor).

No. 220 (m.23), Recorda, Mich.:
Memorandum that William de Braose put in his place John Yweyn, vallett', to receive a letter of obligation of 1,000m. which certain of the Welsh from Gower owed him. Cf. no. 59.

No. 221 (m.73d), Br. Ret., Mich.:
The prince of Wales is to exact £5 1s. 7d. from the goods of the bishop of Bangor, £1 17s. from the chapter of Bangor, £2 2s. from the abbot of Cymmer, £1 12s. 2¼d. from the abbot of Enlli, £1 12s. 6d. from the prior of Precelly and other sums from other North Wales ecclesiastics.

E.368/77   34–35 Edward I   (1306–7)

No. 222 (m.10d), Br. d. Bar., Mich.:
Two writs concerning payments by the prior of Coventry into the Wardrobe at Rhuddlan.

No. 223 (m.51), D.d., Pascha:
A day for account is given to John Grey to reply concerning the value of the lands of Urian de Sancto Petro. He will reply for the Welsh lands to the prince of Wales.

No. 224 m.53), Br. d. Bat., Trin.: Carlisle, 6 May 1307:
Welsh hostages (Norfolk and Suffolk). Cf. appendix I. (E.159/80, m.100 Prec. super Comp., Pascha.)

E.159/80 35 Edward I (1306–7)

No. 225 (m.43), Recorda, Pascha:
Ralph Sandwich, constable of the Tower, is given allowances for Welsh prisoners.

No. 226 (m.88), Br. Ret., Mich.:
Order to the preceptor of the Templars in Wales to certify how much wool he sold to John Tumbrie, merchant.

EDWARD II

E.368/78   1–2 Edward II   (1307–8)

No. 227 (m.27d), Fines, Mich.:
Memorandum that William Rongate, chamberlain of West Wales, has been put in the Tower for arrears. Cf. also *infra* (m.78), Fines, Hil., manucaption for him. Accounts, 1303–6 in M. Rhys, *Ministers' Accounts for West Wales, 1277–1306*, pp. 236–441.

No. 228 (m.52d), Br. d. Bar., Pascha: Westminster, 16 May 1308:
Gruffydd and Cynan ap Maredudd are to be paid 19m. a year of the farm of the manor of Edenstowe (Notts) for life.

No. 229 (m.73, 73d), Recorda, Trin.; (m.91d), Br. Ret., Mich.:
Hugh Sprotton, constable of Rhuddlan, is attached to reply to six charges of misusing his position including the use of royal pasture for his own sheep, employing men working on the castle for his own works and of appropriating royal land. He denies all charges and the case is not brought to a verdict.

No. 230 (mm.82d, 100), Br. Ret., Trin.:
The bishop of Bangor, collector of the Fifteenth, is to send £25 to Robert Haselwell for Welsh foot soldiers in Scotland.

E.159/81   1–2 Edward II   (1307–8)

No. 231 (m.46), Recogn., Pascha:
Recognizance that the prior of Llanthony Prima owes Bartholomew Badlesmere £60. (E.159/84, m.46.)

E.368/79   2–3 Edward II   (1308–9)

No. 232 (m.93d), D.d., Trin.:
Walter Pedirton, controller of South Wales, puts as his attorneys to account John Pencock, John Gentilcors and Maurice de Newcastle against William Rongate and William le Here.

No. 233 (m.112), Br. Irr., Trin.:
Thomas Esthall, chamberlain of North Wales, is to deliver what money he has to Roger Wellesworth.

No. 234 (m.115d), Br. Ret., Mich.:
A day for account is given to Thomas Esthall, chamberlain of North Wales. Cf. also *infra*, m.118: the justice is to attend with his rolls.

No. 235 (m.116d), *ibid*:
The justice of Wales is to obtain the proceeds of the Templar lands in South and West Wales and is to deliver them to the chamberlain of South and West Wales. Cf. also *infra*, m.120d, Hil.

No. 236, *ibid*:
Three writs to Hugh Northwood, custodian of the cocket seal in Haverford.

No. 237 (m.122), *ibid*, Pascha:
The justice is to distrain the collectors of the clerical subsidy in the diocese of St. Asaph.

No. 238 (m.127), St. et Vis., Hil.:
View of the account of the prior of Goldcliff, collector of the Fifteenth in the diocese of Llandaff.
Sum due: £138 4s. 3¾d.
Paid: £130 14s.
Owes: £7 10s. 3¾d.
(E.159/82, m.110, St. et Vis., Hil.)

No. 239, *ibid*:
View of the account of Matthew of Nevyn and Adam Goch, collectors of the Fifteenth in Bangor diocese.
Sum due: £60 19s. 0¾d.
Paid to the sheriff of Salop: £47.
After other allowances owes £7.

No. 240 (m.136), *ibid*, Trin.:
View of the account of Elias Puger for Striguil, Chepstow and other lands of the late Roger Bigod, earl of Norfolk. (E.159/82, m.107, audit.)

E.159/82   2–3 Edward II   (1308–9)

No. 241 (m.111), St. et Vis., Hil.:
View of the account of the collectors of the Fifteenth, St. Asaph diocese.
Sum due: £96 14s. 5d.
Paid to the sheriff of Shropshire: £67 13s. 4d.
Paid to Robert Haselwell, royal clerk, for the expenses of certain Welsh foot: £11.
After other allowances owe £5.

No. 242, *ibid*:

View of the prior of Cardigan, collector of the Fifteenth in the archdeaconry of Cardigan.
Sum due: £33 8s.
£26 13s. 1d. allegedly paid to the bishop of St. David's.
Owes £6 14s. 11¾d.
(E.159/82, m.111.)

E.368/80   3–4 Edward II   (1309–10)

No. 243 (m.17), Recorda, Mich.:

Henry Yonger, keeper of victuals at Llanbadarn Fawr, is freed from the Fleet prison in order to come to account. (E.159/83, m.39.)

No. 244 (m.41), D.d., Hil.:

A day for account is given to William Rongate, chamberlain of West Wales.

No. 245 (m.95), Br. Irr., Trin.:

The justice is to levy the arrears from the sub-collectors of the Triennial Tenth in the bishopric of St. David's.

No. 246 (m.96), Br. Ret., Mich.:

The justice is to make enquiry into the corn left in the vacant bishopric of Bangor and deliver it to the chamberlain of North Wales for the king's use.

No. 247, *ibid*:

The justice is to exact £150 from the properties in Haverford of John Cokay and Richard Parmenter, customs collectors.

No. 248, *ibid*:

Writs to the collectors of the clerical Biennial Tenth including Wales.

No. 249 (m.114d), St. et Vis., Hil.:

View of the account of the prior of Llanthony Prima, collector of the Biennial Tenth in the archdeaconries of St. David's and Brecon.
Sum due: £124 13s. 4½d.
Paid to the bishops of Lincoln and London: £38.
Owe: £86 13s. 4½d.
(E.159/83, m.83.)

No. 250, *ibid*:

View of the account of the abbot of Margam, collector of the Biennial Tenth in the diocese of Llandaff. Owes £3 0s. 6d. (E.159/83, m.87d.)

E.159/83   3–4 Edward II   (1309–10)

No. 251 (m.105), Br. Ret., Mich.:
Writs to the constables of North Wales castles about assuring adequate supplies for their garrisons.

E.368/81   4–5 Edward II   (1310–11)

No. 252 (m.93d), Br. Ret., Hil.:
Writs to the collectors of the clerical Tenth (including Wales).

No. 253 (m.95), *ibid*:
Summons to account of William le Here, chamberlain of South Wales. Cf. also nos. 254, 261, 302. (E.159/84, m.100d, Recorda, Pascha.) E.368/82, m.28d, D.d., Mich.

No. 254 (m.95d), *ibid*:
Walter Pedirton is assigned to hear the account of William le Here, chamberlain of South Wales, who is on point of death. Cf. nos. 261, 302.

E.159/84   4–5 Edward II   (1310–11)

No. 255 (m.15), Br. d. Bar., Mich.: Lessuden, 21 September 1310:
The prior of Llanthony Prima is sued to return the money and property taken from the vicar of Gladoc.

No. 256 (m.21d), *ibid*, Hil.: Berwick on Tweed, 4 February 1311:
Otto Grandison is quit of a £120 debt of Edward I's reign because of his expenses in sending corn from Ireland to Wales for the provisions of castles.

E.368/82   5–6 Edward II   (1311–12)

No. 257 (m.32d), Recorda, Hil.:
Memorandum concerning the failure of Thomas Esthall to account. He is freed from prison. Cf. also *infra*, m.64d, Fines, Trin., manucaption. (E.159/85, m.47d, Recorda, Hil.)

No. 258 (m.85), Br. Irr., Mich.:
William le Here is to deliver the issues of the chamberlainship of South Wales. (E.159/85, m.55, Recorda, Pascha; m.59d, Recorda, Trin.; m.76d, D.d., Mich.; m.99d, Br. Irr., Mich.)

No. 259 (m.101), St. et Vis., Mich.:
Audit of the account of William Leyburn (for 1292) for the farm of the castle of Montgomery. (E.159/85, m.82.)

No. 260 (m.104), *ibid*, Hil.:
View of the account of the abbot of Tintern, sub-collector of the clerical Tenth in the bishopric of Llandaff.
Owes £207 6s. 5¼d. for the first year of the reign. Does not reply for the other two years.
Paid to the chief collectors: £195 13s. 10½d.
Put in respite: £6 13s. 4d.
Owes: £4 19s. 2½d.

No. 261 (m.109), *ibid*, Trin.:
Audit: William le Here, chamberlain of West Wales, 29 September 1309 to 25 August 1311.
Sum due: £4,838 4s. 4¾d.
Claims for allowances included £1,628 19s. 10½d. spent on castles, and £430 11s. 1d. paid to Welsh infantry in the king's service.
After allowances owed £2,633 15s. 10¾d.
Paid £2,293 13s. 6d. and owes £340 2s. 4¼d. (E.159/85, m.89d, St. et Vis., Trin.)
Cf. nos. 253, 254, 302.

E.159/85   5–6 Edward II   (1311–12)

No. 262 (m.4), Comm., Mich.:
The justice is to reply to those things which pertain to the chamberlain of North Wales.

No. 263 (m.77), D.d., Pascha:
A day for account is given to the prior of Carmarthen, collector of the clerical Moiety and the clerical Tenth.

E.368/83   6–7 Edward II   (1312–13)

No. 264 (m.39d), Br. d. Bar., Hil.: Windsor, 8 February 1313:
Allowance to be made in his account to William le Here of a reasonable sum as his fee.

No. 265 (m.80), D.d., Pascha:
A day for account is given to William le Here, chamberlain of South Wales.

No. 266 (m.127), Br. Irr., Pascha:
£300 assigned out of the revenue of the chamberlainship of North Wales to Henry Nasard, merchant, for money lent by him for provisions. (E.159/86, m.136.)

No. 267 (m.127d), *ibid*:
440m. assigned to Bartholomew of Lucca from the issues of South Wales. (E.159/86, m.136d.)

No. 268 (m.145d), St. et Vis., Mich.:
Notice that Richard of Oswestry and Anian of Bromfield, collectors of the Fifteenth in St. Asaph diocese, are quit in their account. (E.159/86, m.115d.)

No. 269 (m.147), *ibid*, Hil.:
Audit of Matthew Nevyn and Adam Goch, collectors of the Fifteenth in the Bangor diocese. (E.159/86, m.116d.)

E.159/86 6–7 Edward II (1312–13)

No. 270 (m.91), Fines, Mich.:
Manucaption for Thomas Cheddesworth, chamberlain of North Wales.

No. 271 (m.100d), D.d., Mich.:
Summonses to the chief collectors in Wales of the ecclesiastical Moiety and Tenths.

E.368/84 7–8 Edward II (1313–14)

No. 272 (m.40), D.d., Mich.:
Adjournment of the account of William le Here, chamberlain of South Wales.

No. 273 (m.41), *ibid*:
David, bishop of St. David's, puts in his place to account as collector of the Fifteenth, Henry de Woolhampton, chaplain of Richard Bray. (E.159/87, m.115d.)

No. 274 (m.52), Fines, Hil.:
Manucaption for Thomas Esthall, chamberlain of North Wales. (E.159/87, m.108.)

No. 275 (m.95), Recorda, Trin.:
Ingelram Berengar, custodian of Glamorgan, on 28 October delivered his seal to Bartholomew Badlesmere. (E.159/87, m.133d.)

No. 276 (m.130d), Recogn., Trin.:
John Sandale, Robert Baynard, Antonio Pessagno, William Trente, John Vanne, William Combemartym, William Servat, John Burford and William Doncaster made recognizances of debt of 120m. to the bishop of St. David's; 100m. to the bishop of Llandaff; 60m. to the bishop of Bangor; 100m. to the bishop of St. Asaph. (E.159/87, m.72d.)

No. 277 (m.132), Br. Irr., Mich.:
The prior of Carmarthen is to pay £135 6s. of his revenue as chamberlain of South Wales to Richard Lovel. (E.159/87, m.134.)

No. 278 (m.136), *ibid*, Hil.:
The justice of Wales is to distrain Thomas Esthall, chamberlain of North Wales, because he has not accounted for some time.

No. 279 (m.136d), *ibid*:
Assignment of 200m. from the chamberlain of West Wales to Bartholomew of Lucca. (E.159/87, m.163.)

No. 280 (m.137d), *ibid*:
£15 is assigned to Thomas Blount, keeper of Dolforwyn Castle, out of the issues of the chamberlainship of West Wales.

No. 281 (m.147d), Br. Ret., Mich.:
The prior of Carmarthen, collector of the Fifteenth, is to be distrained for arrears of £34 17s. 9¾d.

No. 282 (m.155), *ibid*, Trin.:
The justice of Wales is to bring the counter-rolls of North Wales so that the chamberlain, Thomas Esthall, can account. (E.159/87, Br. Irr., Hil.)

E.159/87 7–8 Edward II (1313–14)

No. 283 (m.28), Br. d. Bar., Pascha: Torksey, 22 April 1314:
The bishop of Bangor is quit of paying the Tenth because of the destruction of his goods in the recent war. Cf. no. 286.

No. 284 (m.123), D.d., Pascha:
Anian, bishop of Bangor, puts Hugh of Bristol in his place to account for the clerical Moiety and the clerical Tenth.

No. 285 (m.157d), Br. Ret., Mich.:
The bishop of Bangor is to be distrained for the arrears of the clerical Tenth and the clerical Moiety in the diocese of Bangor.

No. 286 (m.160d), *ibid*, Trin.:
The Exchequer is to ascertain if the Welsh dioceses could not pay their taxes because of the devastation and burning in the recent war. Cf. no. 283.

E.368/85 8–9 Edward II (1314–15)

No. 287 (m.34). Br. d. Bar., Hil.:
Rent of two dogs remitted to Paulyn of Cardiff. (E.159/88, m.32, Br. d. Bar., Hil.)

No. 288 (m.39), *ibid*: Westminster, 10 February 1315:
Allowance of £50 to Philip ap Howel, bailiff of Builth, paid to Roger Mortimer of Wigmore for the latter's service in Gascony.

No. 289 (m.40), *ibid*: Westminster, 8 February 1315:
Allowance given in his account to the prior of Carmarthen as chamberlain of South Wales.

No. 290 (m.47), *ibid*: Windsor, 16 April 1315:
40m. allowed to Thomas Cheddesworth, chamberlain of Caernarvon, in his account for wages.

No. 291 (m.60d), Fines, Hil.:
An assessment of the expenses of cleaning out the moat of Caernarvon castle. (E.159/88, m.161d, Fines, Hil.)

No. 292, D.d., Hil.:
A day for account is given to Bartholomew Badlesmere, custodian of Glamorgan. (E.159/88, m.173, D.d., Hil.)

No. 293 (m.165), *ibid*, Trin:
Thomas Esthall is put in the Fleet prison for not submitting his account as chamberlain of North Wales. (E.159/88, m.180, D.d., Trin.) Cf. nos. 278, 282.

No. 294 (m.180), Recogn., Hil.:
A recognizance is enrolled between the prior of Carmarthen, John Pecock of the county of Carmarthen, Richard Wymot of the counties of Pembroke and Carmarthen and John Scudamore of Cardiganshire that they owe Walter Waldeshef, chief butler of the king, £377 14s. 8d., to be paid in instalments.

No. 295 (m.208), Br. Ret., Mich.:
Writs to the justice of Wales to bring to account the prior of Carmarthen, chamberlain of South Wales, and Thomas Cheddesworth, chamberlain of North Wales.

No. 296 (m.209), *ibid*:
Writ to Roger Mortimer, justice of Wales, to collect 11m. and 5s. from the burgesses of Beaumaris for renewing their charter.

No. 298 (m.211), *ibid*:
William Rongate, chamberlain of South Wales, is summoned to account.

No. 299 (m.213r and 213d), *ibid*:
Detailed list of ecclesiastical tax collectors to be brought to account by the justice of Wales. (E.159/88, m.212, Br. Ret., Trin.)

No. 300 (m.215d), *ibid*, Hil.:
Writ to the justice of Chester to exact £80 from the burgesses of Rhuddlan.

No. 301 (m.231d), St. et Vis., Mich.:
Audit: prior of Carmarthen, collector of the clerical Moiety of 1294–5 in the archdeaconries of Carmarthen and Cardigan.
Sum due: £405 17s. 2½d.
Paid: £20 10s. 4d.
For the balance of £285 6s. 10½d. delivered to the marshal of the Exchequer on 20 October 1314 and then freed by pledge of sureties. (E.159/88, mm.185d, 189d.) Cf. nos. 363, 401, 412, 427, 442.

No. 302, *ibid*:
Audit: William le Here, chamberlain of South Wales, 29 September 1307 to 25 August 1311.
Sum due: £3,568 11s. 2½d.
After allowances, owes £317 8s. 11½d. Subsequently another £122 17s. 9d. allowed. But £41 12s. 2d. which he claimed to have paid to Walter Pedirton, justice of Wales, is not allowed, because he failed to produce a mandate warranting payment. £152 18s. 3¾d. of fines and other dues remained uncollected. Cf. nos. 254, 261.
Subsequently he died and the king ordered the seizure of his goods. (E.159/88, mm.185d, 189d.) Account, S.C.6/1218/6 and 7; Enrolled Account, E.372/159, m.36.

No. 303 (m.233d), *ibid*:
View: Thomas Esthall, chamberlain of North Wales, 29 September 1305 to 29 September 1310.
Sum due: £2,642 11s. 1½d.
Committed to the Fleet prison, 23 November 1314.
(E.159/88, m.187.) Cf. nos. 356, 377, 652, 681–4.
Enrolled Account for 29 September 1305 to 29 September 1307 in *B.B.C.S.* 16 (1955), pp. 111–33, from E.372/176, mm.53, 54 (for 1305–12).
Account, 29 September 1305 to 29 September 1312, S.C.6/1211/2a and 2b. Cf. also S.C.6/1211/4 and 5.

No. 304 (mm.235r, 235d, 236), *ibid*:
Audit: Thomas Cheddesworth, chamberlain of North Wales, 29 September 1312 to 29 September 1314.
(This audit was not completed, different figures being given in the second audit, m.236r *infra*.)
First audit (m.235d):
Sum due: £3,086 1s. 3½d. Followed by a view for 29 September 1314 to 5 January 1315—sum due: £148 1s. Combined total: £3,234 2s. 3½d.
Second audit (m.236r) for the same period:
Sum due: £2,327 2s. 6½d. Followed by a view (*ut supra*)—sum due: £148 1s. Combined total: £2,475 5s. 6½d.
Allowances included £194 13s. paid to Roger Mortimer (of Chirk), John Cromwell and John Charlton, leaders of 2,213 Welsh infantry for the war against Scotland, 1314.
After allowances owes £264 11s. 3¼d. (accounted for in a later account, cf. no. 558).
(E.159/88, m.189, St. et Vis., Hil.)
Account, S.C.6/1211/6; Enrolled Account, E.372/159, m.40.

No. 305 (m.235d), *ibid*, Hil.:
Audit: prior of Carmarthen, chamberlain of South Wales, 25 August 1311 to 29 September 1314.
Sum due: £1,513 7s. 3¾d.
Allowances included £91 14s. 6d. paid to Roger Mortimer (of Chirk) and other leaders of Welsh troops going to Newcastle on Tyne.
After allowances owes £377 14s. 8¾d.
Paid on 25 February 1315, day of completion of accounting. (E.159/88, m.189d.)
Account, S.C.6/1219/1; Enrolled Account, E.372/159, m.37.

E.159/88   8–9 Edward II   (1314–15)

No. 305a (m.106d), Recogn., Hil.:
A recognizance is enrolled between Gruffydd ap Maredudd and Cynan his brother for the farm of the manor of Edenstowe (co. Nottingham).

No. 306 (m.130d), Recorda, Mich.:
William Brown, bailiff of the Queen in the commote of 'Meney' (Menai) and amobrarius of the Queen in South Wales renders account.

No. 307 (m.212), Br. Ret., Trin.:
The justice of South Wales is to collect £152 9s. 0½d. from the estates of the prior of Carmarthen, collector of the Tenth in St. David's diocese. The dean and chapter of Bangor are to be similarly distrained for £113 4s. 9½d. of the arrears of the Tenth.

E.159/89   9–10 Edward II   (1315–16)

In this year the K.R. roll is the fuller and has been used as the base, with cross-references to the L.T.R. roll (E.368/86).

No. 308 (m.27d), Br. d. Bar., Hil.: King's Clipston, 1 December 1315:
The bishop of Bangor is made quit of his arrears as tax collector in the reign of Edward I. On account of the rebellion of the Welsh he had been unable to collect the taxes. Cf. no. 412.

No. 309 (m.45), *ibid*, Pascha: Privy Seal, Westminster, 17 May 1316:
Roger Damory is granted £100 for good service in Glamorgan against the king's enemies there.

No. 310 (m.45d), *ibid*: Westminster, 16 May 1316:
Concerning the rights of the priory of Wigmore.

No. 311 (m.49d), Br. d. Bar., Trin.: Westminster, 12 June 1316:
Matilda, widow of the late Gilbert de Clare, earl of Gloucester, is not to be harassed for the debts owed on Gilbert's lands.

No. 312 (m.110), Fines, Mich.:
Manucaption for William Duyn, chamberlain of North Wales, 9–10 Edward II. Account, S.C.6/1211/8.

No. 313 (m.117), D.d., Mich.:
Mandate to John Grey, justice of North Wales, to distrain Anian, bishop of Bangor, collector of the Moiety (of 1294).

No. 314 (m.119), *ibid*:
Further prorogation of the account of Thomas Esthall, chamberlain of North Wales. Cf. nos. 278, 282, 293, 303, 356.

No. 315 (m.123d), D.d., Hil.:
A day for account is given to the prior of Llanthony, collector of the Moiety (of 1294). He replied that he could not account because on account of the war any attempt to levy the tax would have meant the burning of the properties pertaining to his benefices, and that he would bring a petition in the next parliament. Cf. nos. 363, 442.

No. 316 (m.127), *ibid*, Pascha:
Temporary remission of debts for the bishop of Bangor, the prior of Carmarthen and Thomas of Haverfordwest, sub-collectors of the Tenth.

No. 317 (m.164d), Br. Ret., Hil.:
John Giffard, custodian of Glamorgan, is to obtain from the collectors the fines extracted from those who had taken part in the Llywelyn Bren rising; the money is to be sent to the Exchequer and used to expel the Scots who are invading England. For this purpose it is to be given into the custody of John Walwayn. Cf. nos. 324, 352.

No. 318 (m.166), *ibid*, Mich.:
Writ 'sicut pluries' to John Grey, justice of Wales, to distrain the bishop of Bangor for arrears of the Moiety (of 1294). Cf. nos. 308, 412.

No. 319 (m.168), *ibid*, Pascha:
The dean and chapter of St. Asaph are to be distrained for arrears of a clerical tax.
The justice is to distrain the priors of Llanthony, Kidwelly and Carmarthen, collectors of clerical taxes in St. David's diocese.

Additional L.T.R. *entries* (E.368/86):

No. 320 (m.4d), Comm., Mich.:
The office of receiver of Glamorgan is to be handed over to Nicholas de Clare, the rightful custodian.

No. 321 (m.40d), D.d., Mich.:
Adjournment of the account of Welsh officials because of other business (listed) which they have to carry out for the King.

No. 322 (m.43d), *ibid*:
A day for account is given to Richard de Clare and Richard Rodeneye, custodians of the lands of the late Gilbert de Clare, earl of Gloucester.

No. 323 (m.181d), Br. Ret., Mich.:
The above (as in no. 322) are to render account for the estates of Gilbert de Clare under penalty of £100.

E.368/87   10–11 Edward II   (1316–17)

No. 324 (m.5), Comm., Mich.:
Letters patent under the Exchequer seal appointing John Walwayn and Rhys ap Howel to conduct in the lands of the late Gilbert de Clare, earl of Gloucester, in Glamorgan, the levy of the fines imposed in the court of William Montague and his fellow justices in 9 Edward II. The fines were 'for the redemption of the lives and goods' of those involved in the recent rebellion. (E.159/90, m.3d.) Cf. nos. 317, 352.

No. 325 (m.54), Attorn., Hil.:
Writ to Hugh Audley, constable of Montgomery castle, to come and make his claim for the expenses of his custody.

No. 326 (m.67), Br. d. Bar., Pascha: Windsor, 12 May 1317:
Allowance of 2d. a day made to Bartholomew Burghersh for keeping Welsh hostages, as the result of a petition from the men of Glamorgan, that they be properly maintained.

No. 327, *ibid*: Windsor, 10 May 1317:
List of wages to be paid to Glamorgan officials. (E.159/90, m.42). In *C.P.R. 1313–17*, p. 407.

No. 328 (m.68), *ibid*: Windsor, 15 May 1317:
Llywelyn ap Gruffydd sues for 8 marcates of land promised to him by Gilbert de Clare. Bartholomew Burghersh is to deliver to him the annual rent for the years when Gilbert owed it to him. (E.159/90, m.44.)

No. 329, *ibid*: Windsor, 15 May 1317:
Grant of £10 expenses to Robert Grendon, former sheriff, for the time he raised men against the Welsh.

No. 330, *ibid*: Windsor, 15 May 1317:
Grant of 10m. at the request of William Berkeroles for his expenses in keeping the peace during the rising (in South Wales).

No. 331, *ibid* and m.68d: Clarendon, 1 February 1317; Windsor, 15 May 1317:
Wages of 200m. a year granted to Bartholomew Badlesmere for the time he was custodian of Glamorgan.

No. 332 (m.68d), *ibid*: Windsor, 15 May 1317:
Demand by the abbot of Caerleon for allowance for lands he had exchanged with the earl of Gloucester and for which he had not been properly compensated.

No. 333, *ibid*: Windsor, 15 May 1317:
Allowance of 50m. to Payn Turbervill' for keeping the peace in Glamorgan after the tumult which arose after the death of Gilbert de Clare. (E.159/90, m.43.)

No. 334, *ibid*: Windsor, 15 May 1317:
20m. similarly allowed to Leysand d'Avene. (E.159/90, m.43d.)

No. 335, *ibid*: Windsor, 15 May 1317:
£10 similarly allowed to John Norreis. (E.159/90. *ibid*.)

No. 336 (m.80d), *ibid*, Trin.: Westminster, 24 May 1317:
Complaint by the abbot of St. Dogmael's about his excessive assessment to the clerical taxes on his lands. (E.159/90, m.39d.) Cf. no. 382.

No. 337 (m.90d), *ibid*: Privy Seal, Woodstock, 27 June 1317:
Two petitions (not described) have been submitted through John Giffard, custodian of Glamorgan. (E.159/90, m.58d.)

No. 338 (m.159d), Br. Ret., Hil.:
John Giffard and Payn Turbervill, custodians of Glamorgan, to be distrained for failure to account, by two writs.

No. 339 (m.165d), Br. Ret., Pascha:
Prior of Llanthony, collector of the clerical Tenth in St. David's diocese, is to be distrained for failure to account.

No. 340, *ibid*:
The prior of St. John of Jerusalem, Carmarthen, collector in the other half of the diocese, is to be similarly distrained.

No. 341 (m.171d):
View of the account of the collector of the clerical Tenth in the diocese of Llandaff.
Owes £103 8s. 0¾d.
Pays (at Michaelmas) £50; at Easter £20. He is still in debt of £33 8s. 0¾d. and does not answer the justice of Wales who summons him for arrears.

No. 342 (m.173d), *ibid*:
View of the account of the prior and convent of Carmarthen, collectors of the Tenth in the diocese of Carmarthen and Cardigan through Brother Henry Somery. Audit, *infra*, m.192d.
Owes £33 6s. 8d.
Paid (to Roger Mortimer) £20.

E.159/90   10–11 Edward II   (1316–17)

No. 343 (m.17d), Br. d. Bar., Mich.: Scroby, 8 December 1316:
The prior of Swansea complained that the Exchequer was harassing him for taxes on lands which the king had seized (as an alien house).

No. 344 (m.128d), Attorn., Mich.:
The prior of Llanthony appoints as attorneys at his account John Bocklyngton or David Sperman.

No. 345 (mm.157–9d), Br. Ret., Mich.:
The collectors of the Ecclesiastical Tenth and the Moiety in Welsh dioceses are to be distrained. The amounts in question include: the dean and chapter of Bangor for £104 4s. 9½d. for Bangor diocese, and the abbot of Valle Crucis for £13 15s. 4d. for St. Asaph diocese.

E.368/88   11 Edward II   (1317–18)

No. 346 (m.6), Comm., Mich.:
Appointment of Walter Fulburn as chamberlain of South Wales. (E.159/91, m.3.)

No. 347 (m.9d), Br. d. Bar., Mich.:
Receipts under Exchequer seal to the collectors of the clerical Tenth.
To the bishop of Bangor for his diocese (1 October 1317): £38 9s. 7d.
To the bishop of Llandaff for his diocese (14 September 1317): £127 19s. 9d.
To the bishop of St. Asaph for his diocese (8 October 1317): £56.

No. 348 (m.11d), *ibid*: Clipston, 1 December 1316:
Royal mandate to the Exchequer to acquit bishop Anian of Bangor of half a clerical Tenth as the bishopric was in the king's hands when that half was due to be paid. The bishop acknowledges that he owes the other half.

No. 349 (m.54d), *ibid*, Hil.: Westminster, 29 January 1318:
Royal mandate on behalf of the prior of Llanthony, collector of the clerical Tenth. He is not to be distrained for the amounts that he could not collect as he has handed over a list of debtors and their arrears to the bishop of St. David's, in charge of further collection.

No. 350 (m.66), *ibid*: Westminster, 1 March 1318:
A list of the Queen's lands with their values (including Welsh ones). (E.159/91, m.47.)

No. 351 (m.89), Attorn., Pascha:
A day for account is given to Richard Mustlewyk, chamberlain of West Wales. (E.159/91, m.132d.)

No. 352 (m.136d), Br. Irr., Mich.:
Assignment of £322 10s. 10d. to Hugh Despenser out of the fine of the men of Glamorgan. Cf. nos. 317, 324.

No. 353 (m.142d), *ibid*, Pascha:
Walter Fulburn, chamberlain of South Wales, is to pay £100 to John Ycheford and Hugh Colenham, out of the issues of his office.
Edmund Dynieton, chamberlain of North Wales, is to pay the same men £109 14s.

No. 354 (m.148), Br. Ret., Mich.:
Roger Mortimer, justice of Wales, is to come to the Exchequer with the accounts of Thomas Esthall, chamberlain of North Wales.

No. 355 (m.157), St. et Vis., Mich.:
View: Dean and chapter of St. Asaph, sub-collectors of the clerical Tenth in that diocese.
Owe £128 12s. 3d.
After allowances, owe £5 18s. 11d.
Most of it is assigned to William Furneaux, London merchant.

No. 356 (m.165), *ibid*, Pascha:
View: Thomas Esthall, chamberlain of North Wales, 29 September 1305 to 29 September 1310.
Owes (of clear debt) £2,156 11s.
Committed to the Fleet prison, 8 June 1318, and later released on the security of sureties. Cf. nos. 303, 356, 377, 652, 681–4.
Enrolled Account for 29 September 1305 to 29 September 1307 in *B.B.C.S.* 16 (1955), pp. 111–33, from E.372/176, mm.53, 54 (for 1305–12).
Account (1305–12), S.C.6/1211/2a and 2b. Cf. also S.C.6/1211/4 and 5.

No. 357 (m.166), *ibid*, Trin.:
Audits of the collectors of the clerical Tenth.
Bishop of Bangor owes £3 2s. 7d.
Bishop of St. Asaph is quit (E.159/91, m.139d).

E.159/91   11–12 Edward II   (1317–18)

No. 358 (m.8d), Br. d. Bar., Mich.: Privy Seal, Somerton, 10 August 1317:
The auditors are to hear the account of Payn Turbervill', custodian of Glamorgan. (E.159/92, *ibid*, Hil.)

No. 359 (m.132), Attorn., Pascha:
The prior of Kidwelly, collector of the clerical Tenth, St. David's diocese (1314), puts Wilfred Coker as his attorney.

No. 360 (m.165), Br. Ret., Pascha:
The prior of Carmarthen, collector of the clerical Tenth in the archdeaconries of Carmarthen and Cardigan, is to be distrained.

E.368/89   12–13 Edward II   (1318–19)

The corresponding K.R. roll (159/92) has no membrane numbers.

No. 361 (m.8d), Comm., Trin.:
Release of certain rights to the burgesses of Carmarthen in return for a rent of £22 a year.

No. 362 (m.24d), Recorda, Hil.:
Walter Fulburn, chamberlain of South Wales, made a recognizance that he had received £50 from Hugh Northwood, collector of the customs at Haverford.

No. 363 (m.34d), Recorda, Trin.:
Proceedings on the account of the prior of Llanthony Prima, collector of the clerical Moiety (of 1294–5) and of the clerical Tenth (of 1295–6) in the diocese of St. David's. His claim that most of these taxes could not be levied was upheld by inquisition held at Carmarthen in September 1318. The levy was prevented by the notorious war between the king and the Welsh in 1294–5 in the archdeaconries of St. David's and Brecon. These archdeaconries were so devastated and destroyed that of the Moiety only £240 could be collected and of the Tenth only £30 7s. 1¼d. The prior is acquitted by a further mandate of 8 June 1319. *Infra*, m.111d and E.368/93, Recorda, Trin. They appear under the same terms and places on the K.R. roll for this year, which has no membrane numbers. Cf. nos. 301, 315, 412, 427, 442.

No. 364 (m.47d), Fines, Pascha:
William Shalford, controller of the Exchequer at Caernarvon, came and presented the accounts for the castles of Caernarvon, Beaumaris, Criccieth and Harlech. (E.159/92, Fines, Pascha.)

No. 365 (mm.54, 55), Attorn., Hil.:
Gwenllian, wife of the late Payn Turberville, and executor of his will appoints attorneys, Walter Bonevill' and Alexander Rok, to render account for Glamorgan, of which Payn was lately custodian. They claim that they cannot account properly because of the war raised in Wales, and that they can neither levy the money nor should they be burdened with it. They produce schedules of particulars. Hugh Despenser, the Younger, now lord of Glamorgan, is appointed to examine these for possible fraud. Gwenllian comes to the Exchequer but Hugh fails to answer the writ. (E.159/92, Attorn., Hil.) Further writs, E.368/91, m.92d, Br. d. Bar. Turberville's account, S.C.6/1202/8; Enrolled Account E.372/163, m.34.

No. 366 (m.94d), Br. d. Bar., Pascha: York, 25 March 1319:
The descendants of 'Ierwarde le Galeys' sue for the money owed to them from the farm of the manor of Edenstowe. (E.159/92, Br. d. Bar., Hil.)

No. 367 (m.96d), *ibid*: Kirkeham, 10 April 1319:
Allowance made in his account to the sheriff of Norfolk and Suffolk for the expenses of Rhys, brother of Maelgwyn Griffin and his son and Rhys ap Maredudd in prison in Norwich castle.

No. 368 (m.132), Recogn., Hil.:
Recognizance by Hugh Northwood of Haverford of a debt of £4 5s. 8d.

No. 369 (m.147d), *ibid*, Trin.:
Recognizance by Thomas Clarce of Cardigan.

No. 370 (m.150d), Br. Irr., Hil.:
Assignment of 1,000m. each from the revenues of the Exchequers of North and South Wales to Antonio Uso di Mare, merchant (of Genoa). (E.158/92, Br. Irr., Hil.) Cf. no. 386.

No. 371 (m.174), Br. Ret., Pascha:
Peter Hynkele, executor of the will of William Sutton, justice of North Wales, is to come to account.

No. 372, *ibid*:
Ditto for Hugh Audley, late justice of Wales.

No. 373 (m.173d), *ibid*, Pascha:
Hugh Despenser is commissioned to examine the administration of Glamorgan during its recent custody by John Giffard of Brimpsfield. (E.159/92, D.d., Hil.)

No. 374, *ibid*:
The justice of Wales is to enquire into the goods of William of Drogheda.

No. 375 (m.186), St. et Vis., Hil.:
View: Richard Laugharne and Stephen Legh, customs collectors at Haverford and the port of Milford, 10 March 1307 to 13 January 1309. They had paid their revenue of £6 3s. to William Rongate, former chamberlain of West Wales.
View: Hugh Northwood and Robert Cas, customs collectors at Haverford. They had paid £4 5s. 8¾d. to William le Here, late chamberlain of South Wales, and owe ¾d.

No. 376 (m.190), St. et Vis., Trin.:
Audit: William le Duyn, chamberlain of North Wales, 29 September 1315 to 1 May 1317.
Sum due: £2,072 2s. 6d.
Allowances include:
£39 6s. 2½d. spent in 9 Edward II on taking down a certain hall of the king called the Hall of Llywelyn at Conway, transporting it to the castle of Caernarvon and re-erecting it there, including the expenditure on timber and nails.
£54 spent on 1,500 Welsh infantry sent in 10 Edward II to Newcastle on Tyne for service against the Scots.
£100 7s. 3d. paid for the wages of thirty-three Welsh hostages taken in North Wales and detained in Chester castle by the king's order from

29 August 1315. One of the hostages died on 6 March 1317, and the others continued to be detained for the rest of his term of office and beyond it, to 18 October 1317 (cf. no. 398).
After allowances owes £3 17s. 11¼d.
Accounts, S.C.6/1211, nos. 8 and 9. Enrolled Account, E.372/163, m.30.

No. 377 (m.191r and d), *ibid*:
Audit: Thomas Esthall, chamberlain of North Wales, 29 September 1307 to 29 September 1312.
Sum due: £6,169 4s. 4½d.
Also owes £1,350 5s. 5½d. of the remainder of his account as chamberlain of North Wales for the years 29 September 1302 to 29 September 1305.
Allowances claimed by Esthall included:
200 marks paid to 950 Welsh infantry arrayed in North Wales in October 1309 to serve against the Scots (cf. no. 681).
£678 19s. 2d. paid in advance in wages due to 2,150 Welsh infantry sent to serve against the Scots in 2 and 3 Edward II.
After various provisional allowances owed £1,086 4s. 9¼d.
He appeared again at the Exchequer at York in the Michaelmas term following. In the absence of the justice Hugh Audley or of any deputy of Audley no final audit could be made of Esthall's account for the years 29 September 1305 to 29 September 1307, but it was decided by the barons of the Exchequer to make a view of account, by which he owed £142 19s. 8¾d. Combined debt: £1,229 4s. 7d., adjourned for further accounting.
Cf. nos. 303, 356, 681–4.
Account for 29 September 1302 to 29 September 1305, in *B.B.C.S.* 1 (1922), pp. 257–75.
Enrolled Account for 29 September 1305 to 29 September 1307, in *B.B.C.S.* 16 (1955), pp. 111–33.
Accounts, S.C.6/1211/2a, 2b, 4, 5. Enrolled Account, E.372/176, mm.53, 54.

E.159/92   12–13 Edward II   (1318–19)

This roll has no membrane numbers.

No. 378, Comm., Hil.:
Commission to Hugh Northwood and Robert Cas to collect the customs at Haverford.

No. 379, Br. d. Bar., Mich.: York, by writs of 10, 11, 14 (2) and 15 (2) November:
Allowance by six writs of 1318 in his account, made to Richard Mustlewyk, chamberlain of West Wales, for his expenses; including the cleaning of Carmarthen castle and the defence of Dryslwyn castle at the time when Llywelyn Bren rose. Cf. Chanc. Misc., C.47/10/32/15, m.1d.

No. 380, *ibid*: York, 10 November 1318:
An enquiry, as the result of a petition by the abbot of St. Dogmael's, that poverty made it impossible for him to pay his taxes.

No. 381, *ibid*:
The heiress of Owen de la Pole is made quit of rent owed for the township of 'Makentheth' (Machynlleth).

No. 382, *ibid*, Pascha:
Royal mandate to the Exchequer of 17 February 1319 on behalf of the abbot of St. Dogmael's. He has been taxed twice on the same possessions for a clerical tax. He is assessed at £32 11s. 8d. in the diocese of St. David's, but he has also been taxed piecemeal on the same possessions in various places in the archdeaconry of Cardigan. Cf. nos. 336, 379, 395.

No. 383, St. et Vis., Mich.:
Audit: Richard Mustlewyk, chamberlain of West Wales, 5 May 1315 to 29 September 1317.
Sum due: £2,036 9s. 5¼d.
Allowances include £202 10s. paid to Robert Multon assigned in 9 Edward II to array 2,500 Welsh infantry in South Wales for muster at Newcastle on Tyne.
Debt on 6 November 1318: £143 12s. 1½d.
After further allowances in final accounting has a surplus (E.368/89, St. et Vis., Mich.)
Account for 8–9 Edward II, S.C.6/1219/2 ; Enrolled Account, 8–11 Edward II, E.372/162, m.35.

No. 384, *ibid*, Hil.:
Audit of the account of Richard of Laugharne and Stephen Legh, collectors of the new custom in Haverford, and of Hugh Northwood and Robert Cas, collectors of the wool custom at Haverford.

No. 385, Br. Irr., Mich.:
Instructions to Edmund Dynieton, chamberlain of North Wales, to assign £813 3s. 8d. to Roger Mortimer, justice of Wales.

No. 386, *ibid*:
Further assignment to Antonio Uso di Mare (of Genoa) of 2,000m. out of the subsidy granted by the loyal Welshmen in Wales in the recent York Parliament (1318). Cf. no. 370 and appendix II.

No. 387, Br. Irr., Trin.:
Instructions for raising troops in Wales to be sent to Newcastle for service in the Scottish war.

No. 388, Br. Ret., Mich.:
Instructions to justices of North and South Wales for collecting the Welsh subsidy.

E.368/90   13–14 Edward II   (1319–20)

No. 389 (m.10), Recorda, Hil.:
Writ to Edmund Hakelut, constable of Dynefwr castle. The king wishes to know the annual revenue and expenses incurred in the custody of the castle.

No. 390 (m.22), Recorda, Trin.:
An account for Conway castle.

No. 391 (m.37), Fines, Hil.:
Manucaption for debt of William Duyn, chamberlain of North Wales.
(E.159/93, mm.110, 111.) Cf. also E.159/94, mm.136d, 141d, Fines, Hil.

No. 392 (m.38), *ibid*, Pascha:
Manucaption for Thomas Esthall, chamberlain of North Wales. Cf. also
E.368/91, mm.52d, 53, 54, 54d, Fines, Hil.

No. 393 (m.39), *ibid*:
Expenses on Caernarvon castle.

No. 394 (m.50), D.d., Pascha:
Roger Mortimer, justice of Wales, puts William Shalford, controller of
North Wales, as his attorney against Edmund Dynieton, chamberlain of
North Wales.

No. 395 (m.94), Br. d. Bar., Trin.: Westminster, 5 June 1320:
Instructions to the Exchequer in the dispute about the clerical taxation on
St. Dogmael's Abbey. (E.195/93, m.40d, Br. d. Bar., Pascha.) Cf. nos. 336,
379, 382.

No. 396 (m.131), Br. Ret., Hil.:
Summons to Walter Fulburn, chamberlain of South Wales, to account.

No. 397 (m.137), *ibid*, Trin.:
Summons to the prior of Carmarthen, chamberlain of South Wales, to
account. Cf. also E.368/91, m.74, Attorn., Pascha (manucaption for him).

No. 398 (m.151d), St. et Vis., Trin.:
Audit: Edmund Dynieton, chamberlain of North Wales, 3 April 1317 to
8 April 1319.
Sum due: £2,593 3s. 11¾d.
Also accounts for £928 11s. 1d. received from the aid of the Fifteenth
granted by the community of North Wales for the Scottish war in
12 Edward II. Cf. no. 565.
Allowances included:
£11 4s. paid to Roger Mortimer (of Chirk), justice of Wales, for the expenses
of nine men leading Gruffydd ap Rhys from Rhuddlan to Clarendon and
from thence to Chirk.
£171 1s. 4d. paid to John Sapy, constable of Beaumaris, for the wages
of eight mounted men-at-arms and twelve balistarii retained in the castle
for 263 days in 8 Edward II 'occasione quorundam turbacionum in partibus
Wallie per Lewelinum Bren tunc motarum' and nine men (including three
mounted men-at-arms) similarly retained during fifty-nine days in
9 Edward II.

£68 for the wages of thirty-two Welsh hostages in Chester castle between
1 May 1317 and 18 October 1317 at 3d. per day for each hostage. The
payment was made to them through Eynon ap Philip, Cynfrig ap Philip,
Tudur Gam and David ap Howel.
Dynieton claimed to have a surplus of £69 13s. 9¾d.
Accounts, S.C.6/1211/10 and 1212/1. Enrolled Account, E.372/164, m.35.

E.159/93   13–14 Edward II   (1319–20)

No. 399 (m.17), Br. d. Bar., Hil.: York, 25 September 1318:
A complaint by Rhys Maelgwyn that he has been unjustly burdened of a
rent of 10m. for the manor of Dalton-by-Brayenton (Lancs). Endorsed that
he is quit. (E.159/94, m.27.)

No. 400 (m.21d), *ibid*: Swinford, 8 February, 1320:
Exchequer to deal with an accusation of corruption against Henry Shirokes
chamberlain of North Wales. Cf. *infra*, m.83, Recorda, Pascha.

No. 401 (m.42), *ibid*, Trin.:
The barons are to enquire whether the prior of Carmarthen failed to collect
the clerical taxes in Wales (1295–6) on account of the war between the
king's father and the Welsh. Cf. nos. 301, 404, 412, 427, 442.

No. 402 (m.63), Recogn., Trin.:
Recognizance of debt by Rhys ap Gruffydd of 'Llansardon'.

No. 403 (m.75), Recorda, Hil.:
Edmund Hakelut, constable, is not to be burdened in his account for tha
part of Dynefwr castle which has been burnt down. (E.368/91, m.72,
Br. d. Bar., Mich.)

No. 404 (m.93), *ibid*, Trin.:
Concerning the account of the prior of Carmarthen, collector of the clerical
Moiety.

No. 405 (m.98), *ibid*:
Inquisition into properties in the diocese of Llandaff destroyed in the
rebellion of Llywelyn Bren and exoneration of the ecclesiastical tax collector
for failure to collect taxes from these properties.

No. 406 (m.122), D.d., Trin.:
A day for account is given to Henry Shirokes, chamberlain of North Wales.
(E.368/91, m.58d, D.d., Mich.)

No. 407 (m.122d), *ibid*:
The prior of Carmarthen, collector of the Tenth in the diocese of St. David's,
puts Henry Somery as his attorney to render account.

No. 408 (m.123), *ibid*:
A day for account is given to the prior of Carmarthen, the dean and chapter of Bangor and the abbot of Margam to render account for the ecclesiastical Moiety (of 1294) and the Tenth.

No. 409 (m.149), Br. Irr., Trin.:
Henry Shirokes, chamberlain of North Wales, is to levy the £100 owed by the burgesses of Caernarvon.

E.368/91   14–15 Edward II   (1320–21)

No. 410 (m.51d), Fines, Hil.:
Manucaption for William Shalford, controller of North Wales. (E.159/94, m.137d.)

No. 411 (m.62), D.d., Pascha:
A day for account is given to Thomas Cheddesworth, chamberlain of North Wales.

No. 412 (m.73), Br. d. Bar., Mich.:
Royal mandate to the Exchequer of 6 November 1320 ordering an enquiry into the allegations of the bishop of Bangor, collector of the clerical Moiety of 1294–5 and of the clerical Tenth, granted by the clergy in 1295, that he could not collect these taxes in his diocese 'propter diversas depredaciones et combustiones ibidem tam per Anglicos quam per Wallenses factas et etiam guerram inter patrem Regis et prefatos Wallenses'. (E.159/94, mm.15, 17d.) Cf. nos. 308, 420, 427, 442.

No. 413 (m.75), *ibid*: Westminster, 12 November 1320:
Royal mandate to the Exchequer ordering an enquiry into the form and terms of the grant of a Fifteenth conceded to the king in 12 Edward II in North Wales, to be levied from the goods of his tenants there. The bishop of Bangor alleges that the levy did not extend to tenants within liberties. (E.159/94, m.48, Br. d. Bar., Pascha.)

No. 414 (m.76d), *ibid*: Westminster, 8 November 1320:
Allowance to the prior of Carmarthen for money spent repairing Carmarthen castle. *Infra*, m.77d. (E.159/94, m.18d.)

No. 415, *ibid*: Privy Seal, Westminster, 14 November 1320:
Allowance to Roger Damory for his expenses in Scotland and Wales.

No. 416 (m.79d), *ibid*: Westminster, 16 November 1320:
Allowance to Edmund Dynieton for money spent on repairs to Caernarvon castle. (E.159/94, m.22; cf. also, *ibid*, Recorda, Pascha, m.109.)

No. 417 (m.92d), *ibid*, Pascha: Westminster, 18 February 1321:
Allowance in his account as custodian of Glamorgan to be made to Payn Turbervill' for £20 to be paid to a royal envoy. Account, S.C.6/1202/8.

No. 418 (m.136), St. et Vis., Mich.:
Audit: Robert, prior of Carmarthen, chamberlain of South Wales, 2 September 1314 to 5 May 1315.
Sum due: £20 16s. 0¾d.
After allowances owes £14 10s. 6¾d. paid in 1321. (E.159/94, m.144d.)
Account, S.C.6/1219/1. Enrolled Account, E.372/161, m.53.

E.159/94   14–15 Edward II   (1320–1)

No. 419 (m.16d), Br. d. Bar., Mich: Westminster, 6 and 7 November 1320:
Two writs of allowance in his account to William Martin, justice of South Wales, for money paid to the chamberlain of South Wales.

No. 420 (m.48), *ibid*, Pascha: York, 22 May 1319:
Petition by the bishop of Bangor that the church of Llanfaes (Caerns) had been destroyed in the rebellion of Madog ap Llywelyn. Its value was 20s. a year.

No. 421 (m.62), Recogn., Mich.:
The abbot of Whitland made a recognizance of debt of £20 to the abbot of Strode.

No. 422 (m.81d), Recorda, Mich.:
Writ concerning a dispute over the temporalities of St. Dogmael's abbey.

No. 423 (m.123), D.d., Mich.:
A day for account is given to the prior of Carmarthen, collector of the Tenth and the Moiety.

No. 424 (m.123d), *ibid*:
A day is given to the abbot of Margam, collector of the Moiety and the Tenth.

E.368/92   15 Edward II   (1321–2)

The scarcity of entries in this year is probably due to the failure of Welsh officials to account owing to the disorder caused by the civil war in England and Wales.

No. 425 (m.42d), Br. d. Bar., Mich: Westminster, 26 August 1321:
A writ concerning the rights of the bishop of Llandaff in the Wye valley. (E.159/95, m.7d.)

No. 426 (m.49d), *ibid*, Hil.:
Writs concerning the activities of the Mortimers in the Welsh March. In J. Conway Davies, *The Baronial Opposition to Edward II*, appendix, p. 561, where the membrane reference is given as 48d.

No. 427 (m.63), *ibid*, Trin.: York, 5 July 1322:
Complaint by the prior of Carmarthen, collector of the Moiety and Tenth
(1294–5), that he had been able to collect only £35 on account of the
rebellion of Madog ap Llywelyn. (E.159/95, m.33.) Cf. nos. 301, 412, 442.

No. 428 (m.64), *ibid*:
Writ to the barons to examine the accounts of the receivers of the rebels'
lands in the Marches.

No. 429 (m.91), Br. Ret., Trin.:
The prior of Carmarthen, chamberlain of South Wales, to be distrained.

No. 430 (m.96), St. et Vis., Mich.:
Audit: John Giffard of Brimpsfield, custodian of the lands of the late
Gilbert de Clare, earl of Gloucester, in Glamorgan, 20 April 1316 to
22 May 1317.
Sum due: £1,046 7s. 5½d.
Allowances included payments for a huge quantity of provisions and
military equipment for Glamorgan castles, and £199 15s. 9d. paid out over
the expenses of 1,000 Welsh infantry led by Henry Pembridge from Cardiff
to Newcastle on Tyne.
After allowances owed £418 8s. 5d., which the sheriff of Gloucester was
ordered to levy from his possessions. This order cancelled after Easter 1322
as by then Giffard's lands were in the king's hands. (E.159/95, m.104.)
Account, S.C.6/1202/9. Enrolled Account, E.372/165, m.28.

No. 431 (m.97), *ibid*:
Audit: dean and chapter of Bangor, collectors of the clerical Tenth in
their diocese.
Owe £3 2s. 7d.

No. 432, *ibid*:
Audit: abbot of Tintern, collector of the clerical Tenth in the diocese of
Llandaff.
Owes £1 15s. 10¾d.

No. 433 (m.99), *ibid*, Hil.:
Audit: Henry Shirokes, chamberlain of North Wales, 8 April 1319 to
29 September 1320.
Sum due: £2,548 10s. 7½d.
After allowances, on 9 August owed £215 19s. 1d., and withdrew from the
Exchequer without permission.
Orders for the attachment of Shirokes and for the levy of this debt from his
possessions. (E.159/95, m.108, Hil., less complete.) Cf. nos. 524, 527.
Account, S.C.6/1212/2. Enrolled Account, E.372/166, m.30 (ending with
a debt of £877 7s. 5¾d., including various allowances claimed by Shirokes,
but not accepted by the Exchequer).

No. 434 (m.104), *ibid*:
Audit: prior of Carmarthen, collector of the Tenth in St. David's diocese, 14 Edward II.
Owes £41 13s. 2½d.

No. 435 (m.129), Br. Ret., Mich.:
Mandate to the justice of Wales to distrain the abbot of Margam, collector of the Moiety and Tenth.

No. 436 (m.130d), *ibid*:
The abbot of Valle Crucis, collector of the Moiety and Tenth, is to be similarly distrained.

No. 437, *ibid*:
The customs collectors at Haverfordwest are to be distrained for arrears.

E.368/93 16–17 Edward II (1322–3)

No. 438 (m.9d), Comm., Trin.:
The tenants of Roger Mortimer of Wigmore are in future to answer for their lands to the king, in whose hands the lands now are.

No. 439 (m.12d), Recorda, Mich:
Mandate to William Norwich (acting treasurer), to deliver the record of the indictment of the Mortimers.

No. 440 (m.24d), *ibid*, Hil.:
The prior of Carmarthen has failed to account. (E.159/96, m.71d.)

No. 441 (m.33d), *ibid*, Trin.:
Memoranda that the goods of Roger Mortimer of Wigmore and other rebels had been received in the Wardrobe.

No. 442 (m.37d), *ibid* and m.20, Hil.:
The prior of Llanthony is called to account for the clerical taxes of which he was collector in 1294–5. Endorsed that he had been able to collect only £240 of the Moiety 'propter guerram tunc inter Wallenses et dominum regem'. E.159/96, m.89d.) Cf. nos. 315, 363, 427. (Cf. also m.32d.)

No. 443 (m.48), D.d., Mich.:
A day for account is given to Thomas Cheddesworth, chamberlain of North Wales. (E.159/96, m.97.)

No. 444 (m.75), Br. Irr., Trin.:
Writ to Robert Power, chamberlain of North Wales, concerning the victualling of North Wales castles. (E.159/96, m.147d.)

No. 445 (m.76d), Br. Ret., Mich.:
Writs of 16 October requiring William de la Beche to reply concerning the value of the Welsh lands of the rebels (Ceri, Cydewain and Dolforwyn) and 'de omnibus aliis circumstanciis dictam custodiam tangentibus'.
Similar writs to:
Walter le Gras, custodian of Denbigh and Cefnllys.
Robert Morby, custodian of Brecon and property of Humphrey de Bohun.
John Dene, custodian of Blaenllyfni, Bwlchdinas and Pencelly.
Richard Marshal, custodian of Brynllys and the goods of Rhys ap Howel.
Edmund Gocelyn, custodian of Crikhowel and Ystradowen and the goods of Aymery Pauncefoot.
Gruffydd ap Rhys, custodian of Builth and the goods of Humphrey de Bohun.
Humphrey Littlebury, custodian of Radnor and the goods of Roger Mortimer of Wigmore.
Alan Charlton, custodian of Wigmore and property of Roger Mortimer of Wigmore.
Ralph Botiller, custodian of Ludlow and the manor of Lacebury (Stanton Lacy, Salop).
Robert Sapy, constable of Welshpool castle and custodian of Powys.
Accounts for the lands of the contrariants, including specifically Welsh lands, S.C.6/1145, no. 6 (Herefordshire and March of Wales), 7 (earl of Hereford), 16 and 23 (Mortimer lands); 1148/7 (Shropshire and Herefordshire); 1287/2 and 3 (Wales); 1289/5 (diverse).
Enrolled Accounts, E.358/14, 15, 16.

No. 446 (m.78), *ibid*:
Writ to the justice of Wales ordering him to collect the arrears owed to the prior of Carmarthen, collector of the Tenth. (E.159/96, 149d, 161d, Trin., all Welsh clerical tax collectors.)

No. 447 (m.84), *ibid*, Trin.:
The justice of Wales is to bring to account Adam Wetenhale, chamberlain of North Wales.

E.159/96   16–17 Edward II   (1322–3)

No. 448 (m.40), Br. Ret., Trin.:
Allowance in his account made to William Duyn, chamberlain of North Wales, for his expenses repairing North Wales castles.

No. 449 (m.149d), *ibid*, Mich.:
The abbot of Valle Crucis is to be distrained for his arrears as collector of the clerical Tenth.

No. 450 (m.161d), *ibid*, Trin.:
Summons to account to the following clerical tax collectors:
Prior of Carmarthen; abbot and convent of Tintern; abbot and convent of Valle Crucis; dean and chapter of Bangor.

No. 451 (m.43), *ibid*:
Remission of debt to the men of Usk.

No. 452 (m.98), D.d., Hil.:
A day for account given to bishops of St. Asaph and Bangor, collectors of the 'fifth penny in the mark' in their dioceses.

No. 453 (m.100d), *ibid*, Pascha:
A day for account is given to Robert Morby, custodian of the Brecon lands of Roger Mortimer.

E.368/94   17–18 Edward II   (1323–4)

No. 454 (m.22d), Recorda, Mich.:
Record concerning the failure to account of Thomas Esthall and Thomas Cheddesworth, late chamberlains of North Wales.

No. 455 (m.57d), *ibid*, Pascha:
Grant of Brecon, Hay, Huntingdon, Cantref Selyf, Talgarth, Blaenllyfni and Pencelly to Hugh Despenser the Younger. John Walwayn, the custodian, is to hand over these properties.

No. 456 (mm.71d, 72), Recorda, Trin.: (m.176), St. et Vis., Hil.:
View: Adam Wetenhale, chamberlain of North Wales, 29 September 1320 to 23 March 1323.
Sum due: £1,603 8s. 3½d.
Accounting could not be completed in Hilary term because Edmund, earl of Arundel, justice of Wales, had not sent counter-rolls.
Among claims for allowances, Wetenhale alleged that £312 3s. 3¼d. consisted of sums due from various sheriffs.
In Trinity term he was discharged of this debt, and the earl of Arundel sent the counter-rolls.
Allowances also included £53 7s. 3¼d. surcharged for two years for the extent of Penrhos in Anglesey (cf. *infra,* nos. 563, 680). The exaction of this sum has been respited by the royal mandate 'pro eo videlicet quod si levata fuisset dominus Rex nullos haberet ibidem villanos residentes'. Cf. *infra,* m.142d, Br. Irr., Mich.
Account, S.C.6/1212/4. Enrolled Account, E.372/168, m.46. Cf. no. 494.

No. 457 (m.110d), D.d., Trin.:
A day for account is given to Thomas Esthall, chamberlain of North Wales.

No. 458 (m.151d), Br. Irr., Pascha:
Adam Wetenhale, chamberlain of North Wales, summoned to account.

No. 459 (m.154), Br. Ret., Trin.:
Robert Power, chamberlain of North Wales, and the prior of Carmarthen, chamberlain of South Wales, are brought to account for their arrears.

No. 460 (m.155d), *ibid*:
Thomas Duyn, late chamberlain of West Wales, similarly distrained.

No. 461 (m.157), *ibid*:
Writs to the de la Pole family of Powys.

No. 462, *ibid*:
Roger Boroughill distrained to render account for the issues of the liberty of Brecon which belonged to the earl of Hereford.

No. 463 (m.167d), St. et Vis., Mich.:
Audit of the account of Hugh Northwood, customs collector at Haverford. (E.159/97, m.249.)

No. 464 (m.175), *ibid*:
Audit of the account of Robert Morby of the Brecon lands which belonged to Humphrey de Bohun, earl of Hereford, 23 January 1322 to 10 July 1323. (E.159/97, m.256.)

No. 465 (m.175d), *ibid*, Hil.:
Audit of the account of the constable of Dolforwyn, 23 January 1322 to 25 March following.

No. 466 (m.176d), *ibid*:
Audit of the account of the constables of the castles of Denbigh and Cefnllys and the lands of Maelienydd and Gwerthrynion, 23 January 1322 to 30 March 1322. (E.159/97, m.257.)

No. 467 (m.177), *ibid*:
Audit: (Robert) prior of Carmarthen, chamberlain of South Wales, 20 September 1318 to 29 September 1321.
Sum due: £1,528 15s. 11d.
Allowances included £171 6s. 8d. paid for forty men-at-arms and 3,000 infantry with their bedells (of commotes) and standard bearers led by Rhys ap Gruffydd 'valletus regis' to seize into the king's hands the lands of Cantref Mawr, Cantref Bychan, Gower, Narberth and the cantref of Builth, with castles in the same lands, and also the lands of 'Kenylank' and 'Tendour' in 1322.
After allowances owes £442 12s. 2d., which are to be levied from his possessions.
Account (13 Edward II), S.C.6/1219/11 and the counter-roll, 1219/12.
Account (14 Edward II), 1219/14 and the counter-roll 1219/13.
Enrolled Account, E.372/169, m.48. Cf. no. 517.

No. 468 (m.180d), *ibid*, Pascha:
Audit of the account of Alan Charlton of the issues of Wigmore, 20 January 1322 to 30 March 1322.

No. 469, *ibid*:
Audit of the account of Hugh Despenser the Younger for the properties of Hugh Audley the Younger and Margaret, his wife, in Wales and Gloucestershire, 4 October 1322 to 15 April 1324.
Sum due: £272 14s. 8¾d.
(E.159/97, m.261d.)

No. 470 (m.184), *ibid*, Trin.:
Audit: Walter Fulburn, chamberlain of South Wales, 29 September 1317 to 20 September 1318.
Sum due: £477 13s. 7¼d.
After allowances owes £1 5s. 7¾d.
Account, S.C.6/1159/1. Enrolled Account, E.372/168, m.40.

No. 471, *ibid*:
Audit of the account of William de la Beche, constable of the castles of Dolforwyn, Ceri, Cydewain. (E.159/97, m.257.)

E.159/97   17–18 Edward II   (1323–24)

No. 472 (m.9), Comm., Hil:
Writ to the justice of Wales concerning the payment of £35 due from the men of Caernarvon at the Exchequer annually in return for certain rights.

No. 473 (m.20d), Br. d. Bar., Mich.: York, 3 May 1323:
The barons are to make enquiry and judge to what degree the prior and convent of Carmarthen were affected by the war between the Welsh and the English so that, if necessary, they can be exempted from clerical taxes.

No. 474 (m.23d), *ibid*: York, 22 May 1322:
Allowance to Edmund Dynieton, chamberlain of North Wales, of £100 paid to Roger Mortimer of Chirk. (E.159/99, m.49.)

No. 475 (m.223d), D.d., Mich:
The abbot of Tintern appoints as his attorney to account Gerard Johan, merchant of the Bardi.

No. 476 (m.231d), D.d., Hil.:
The prior of Carmarthen appoints as his attorney to account John Wynton, a fellow monk.

No. 477 (m.283d), Br. Irr., Hil.:
The chamberlain of North Wales must repair the North Wales castles out of his revenue.

No. 478, *ibid*:
Identical order to the chamberlain of South Wales.

E.368/95 18–19 Edward II (1324–5)

For the next two years there are separate rolls for the areas north and south of Trent. I have included the Welsh entries from both sets of rolls.

No. 479 (m.34d), Recorda, Hil.:
Earl Warenne's heir is to reply for the £40 per annum rent owed for the custody of Hope.

No. 480 (m.60), Fines, Trin.:
Manucaption for Robert Clement, custodian of Blaenllyfni. (E.159/99, m.156, D.d., Mich.)

No. 481 (m.71d), D.d., Mich:
Rhys ap Gruffydd, custodian of Llandovery castle, appoints as his attorney to account Nicholas Syde for the castles of Newburgh and Llandovery and the lands of Roger Mortimer in West Wales from 13 February 1322 onwards. (E.159/99, m.176d.)

No. 482 (m.114d), St. et Vis., Mich.:
The bishop of St. David's is to distrain Thomas Duyn to make him account at the Exchequer for his chamberlainship of South Wales because Thomas is beneficed in his diocese.

No. 483 (m.124), St. et Vis., Pascha:
Audit of the account of Hugh Northwood and Robert Cas, customs collectors at Haverfordwest. (E.159/99, m.198.)

E.159/99 18–19 Edward II (1324–5)

No. 484 (m.14d), Br. d. Bar., Mich.: The Tower of London, 20 October 1324:
An enquiry is to be made by the barons of the Exchequer on account of a petition made by the abbot of Margam claiming that he cannot pay his taxes on account of damage by the war.

No. 485 (m.220), Br. Ret., Hil.:
The justice of Wales is ordered to distrain the collectors of customs at Haverfordwest.

E.368/96 18–19 Edward II (1324–25)

No. 486 (m.10), Comm., Trin.:
Writ to Edmund, earl of Arundel, justice of Wales, to carry out extents of the lands of Roger Mortimer of Wigmore and Roger Mortimer of Chirk. (E.159/100, m.5d.)

No. 487 (m.13d), Recorda, Mich.:
Summons to John Charlton and Hawys, his wife, concerning the relief due from Owen, heir of Gruffydd ap Gwenwynwyn. Cf. *infra*, m.63, D.d., Mich.

No. 488 (m.21), *ibid*, Hil.:
Postponement of the account of Robert Power, chamberlain of North Wales, as he is at Portsmouth with Welsh troops. (E.159/100, m.89.)

No. 489 (m.61d), Attorn., Mich.:
John Charlton appoints Richard Nottingham as his attorney to present the extent of the lands of William de la Pole.

No. 490 (m.68d), D.d., Trin.:
A day for account is given to Edmund Dynieton, chamberlain of North Wales, and to William de la Bataille and John Arworth to account for the produce in North Wales castles.

No. 491 (m.73), Fines, Trin.:
Manucaption of Thomas Cheddesworth, chamberlain of North Wales. (E.159/100, m.147.)

No. 492 (m.94), Br. Ret., Pascha:
The prior of Carmarthen is to be attached to render account for the chamberlainship of South Wales.
William Duyn is to be similarly attached for the arrears of the chamberlainship of North Wales.

No. 493 (m.101), St. et Vis., Mich.:
Audit: dean and chapter of Bangor for the biennial clerical Tenth in that diocese for both years.
Owes £6 5s. 2d.
Their attorney withdrew from the Exchequer without permission. A levy of the debt was ordered by a writ directed to the justice of North Wales.

No. 494 (mm. 103r, 103d), *ibid*:
Audit: Adam Wetenhale, chamberlain of North Wales, 29 September 1320 to 23 March 1323.
Sum due: £3,469 9s. 5¾d.
Allowances included £163 6s. 8d. paid to Giles de Beauchamp for Welsh troops led by him to the king for service against Scotland. Wetenhale claimed that his expenditure exceeded his receipts. (E.159/100, m.153.) Cf. no. 456.

No. 495 (m.108d), *ibid*, Hil.:
View of the account of William le Waleys, receiver of revenues from the lands of Thomas, earl of Lancaster, and other rebels.

No. 496 (m.115), *ibid*, Trin.:
Audit: Robert Power, chamberlain of North Wales, 23 March 1323 to 29 September 1324.
Sum due: £2,328 2s. 0½d.
After allowances owes £277 16s. 5d. which he claims to be still due from various sheriffs.
£240 paid in October to November 1325.
£37 16s. 5d. paid in May 1327 and is quit.
Accounts, S.C.6/1212/10 and 11. Enrolled Account, E.372/169, m.45.

E.159/100   18–19 Edward II   (1324–25)

No. 497 (m.5d), Comm., Trin.:
Order to make extents of the lands of Roger Mortimer of Chirk and other rebels.

No. 498 (m.16), Br. d. Bar., Mich.: the Tower, 27 October 1324:
The chamberlain of North Wales is to make Rhys Coyke quit of a debt of £15.

No. 499 m.23), *ibid*, Hil.: the Tower, 12 January 1325:
The prior of Swansea is given the king's protection as he is an alien.

No. 500 (m.26d), *ibid*: Langley, 26 January 1325
Writ to the justice of Wales to force the deputies of Henry Shirokes to account as he is unable to do so.

No. 501 (m.44d), *ibid*, Trin.: Westminster, 12 July 1325:
Allowance to Robert Power, chamberlain of North Wales, for money spent on the maintenance of Caernarvon castle.

No. 502, *ibid*:
'Yereward Weyll', tenant of Aberfan, is made quit of rent for life.

No. 503 (m.133d), D.d., Mich.:
Adam Wetenhale, chamberlain of North Wales, put in his place to account Gilbert de Bevenyl and Walter Coumb.

No. 504 (m.142d), D.d., Trin.:
Edmund Dynieton appoints William de la Bataille as his attorney to account.

No. 505 (m.153d), St. et Vis., Mich.:
Account of expenses on Criccieth castle.

E.368/97   19–20 Edward II   (1325–6)

No. 506 (m.10d), Comm., Mich.:
Richard Dowystowe to be distrained by the justice of Wales for 5 marks. Cf. *infra*, mm.103, 108, Br. Ret., Mich.

No. 507 (m.13d), *ibid*:
The lands and goods of Peter Hakelut, rebel, are to be taken into the king's hands. (E.159/101, m.4d.)

No. 508 (m.22), Comm., Trin.:
Enquiry is to be made into the issues of the castles of Cefnllys and Dynefwr and the cantref of Maelienydd. (E.159/102, m.26.)

No. 509 (m.73d), *ibid*:
Thomas Duyn, clerk associated with the chamberlain of South Wales, put Henry Carreu in his place to account.

No. 510 (m.75d), *ibid*:
Gruffydd ap Rhys puts John Penynton in his place to account for the lands of Humphrey de Bohun, the Mortimers, Rhys ap Howel and Aymery Pauncefoot. (E.159/101, m.203d, D.d., Pascha, and m.214d, St. et Vis., Trin.)

No. 511 (m.105d), Br. Ret., Trin.:
Writ concerning the debt owed from the farm of various marcher castles.

No. 512 (m.106), *ibid*:
The prior of Carmarthen, chamberlain of South Wales, and Thomas Duyn, clerk associated with him, had failed to send to the Exchequer the money in their custody because of the dangers of the roads. The king tells them to despatch it quickly. Cf. no. 518.

No. 513 (m.109), *ibid*:
View of the account of Robert Clement, keeper of Blaenllyfni castle and of the lands of Roger Mortimer of Chirk.

No. 514 (m.110), *ibid*:
Audit of the account of Richard Wroth, custodian of Swansea. (E.159/101, m.297.)

No. 515, *ibid*:
Audit: abbot of Tintern, collector of the second year of the biennial clerical Tenth in the diocese of Llandaff.
Owes £14 10s. 2¾d.
After 20 November 1325 there remained a debt of £9 6s. 10¾d., which is to be levied from his possessions.

No. 516 (m.111), *ibid*:
Audit of the account of John Stephen and Robert Cas, customs collectors at Haverford, 7 April 1325 to 29 September 1325. (E.159/101, m.298.)

No. 517 (m.117), *ibid*:
Audit of the account of the prior of Carmarthen and Thomas Duyn, clerk associated with him, 20 September 1318 to 29 September 1321.
Sum due: £1,537 4s. 2½d.
After allowances owes £371 19s. 10½d. which are to be levied from his possessions. Cf. no. 467. Accounts, S.C.6/1219/11 and 14. Counter-rolls, 1219/12 and 13. Enrolled Account, E.372/169, m.48.

E.518 (m.117d), St. et Vis., Trin.:
Audit: Robert, prior of Carmarthen, chamberlain of South Wales, and Thomas Duyn, associated with him in the same office, 29 September 1321 to 29 September 1325.
Sum due: £1,584 16s. 2¼d.
After allowances owe £1,396 10s. 2¼d.
They claimed that around 1,000m. of this sum is deposited in Carmarthen castle which they did not dare to transport to the Exchequer 'propter viarum discrimina' (cf. no. 512).
Paid £494 13s. in July 1326 and £84 on 27 May 1327.
Account for the rest in a later account. Cf. no. 560.
Accounts, S.C.6/1220/1 and 2. Enrolled Account, E.372/171, m.35.

E.159/101   19–20 Edward II   (1325–6)

No. 519 (m.52), Br. d. Bar., Hil.: Bisham, 9 June 1325:
A ship sent by the prior of Carmarthen to victual South Wales castles had been captured by the Scots. Cf. *infra*, m.78.

No. 520, *ibid*: Westminster, 11 June 1325:
Grant to Hugh Despenser the Younger of the castle and town of Dryslwyn and of Cantrefmawr in Wales in exchange for a loan.

No. 521 (m.59d), *ibid*, Pascha: Barnsley, 3 May 1326:
Inquiry into the running of the castle of Haverford granted to Richard Perrers.

No. 522 (m.232d), Br. Ret., Mich.:
Order to distrain the abbot of Valle Crucis, sub-collector of the clerical Tenth, for the arrears in his account.

E.368/98   19–20 Edward II   (1325–6)

No. 523 (m.20), Recorda, Mich.:
William Rongate, chamberlain of South Wales, is put in the Fleet prison for arrears of 1,700m.

No. 524 (m.21), *ibid*:

Henry Shirokes owes £215 19s. 11d. and is to be attached by the sheriffs of Notts and Derby, York and Northumberland. He is put in the Fleet prison. Comes to the Exchequer to bring sureties and is returned to the Fleet. Cf. nos. 433, 527.

No. 525 (m.29), *ibid*:

The prior of Llanthony is exonerated of a debt.

No. 526 (m.93), Br. Ret., Trin.:

Instructions to Richard, bishop of Bangor, to collect the rest of the Tenth owing in his diocese.

No. 527 (m.99d), St. et Vis., Hil:

View: Henry Shirokes, chamberlain of North Wales (no dates given, but it concerns the account for 8 April 1319 to 29 September 1320).
Charged in E.372/169, Ebor. d., with £299 12s. 9¼d.
Committed to the Fleet prison and his debts ordered to be levied from his benefices. Amount due reduced to £182 9s. 11d. and exaction respited to Easter term 1327. Cf. nos. 433, 524. Account, S.C.6/1212/2.

E.159/102 19–20 Edward II (1325–6)

No. 535 (m.26), Comm., Trin.:

Confiscation of the goods of Edmund of Woodstock, earl of Kent, in Wales and elsewhere.

No. 536 (m.40d), Br. d. Bar., Mich.: Westminster, 26 November 1325.

Plea by Henry Shirokes to be freed from the burden of the arrears of the chamberlainship of North Wales which are really the responsibility of Adam Wetenhale.

No. 537 (m.50d), *ibid.*, Hil.: Westminster, 9 July 1325:

Allowance to the chamberlain of South Wales for money spent on South Wales castles. (North Wales—cf. *infra*, m.60, *ibid.*, Trin.)

No. 538 (m.59d), *ibid*, Trin.: Hayles, 2 May 1326:

Allowance in his account to Thomas Cheddesworth, chamberlain of North Wales, for building a stable for the horses of the justice and his entourage when they visit Caernarvon.

No. 539 m.64), *ibid*, Pascha: the Tower, 18 June 1326:

Instructions for dealing with animals offered by the community of North Wales in payment of a debt. Cf. *infra*, m.205d.

No. 540 m.65), *ibid*, Trin.: Privy Seal, the Tower, 26 June 1326:
Custody of the castle of Haverfordwest and of its seal to be handed over to Richard Perrers. Cf. also *infra*, m.124d, Recorda, Trin.: instructions for the manufacture of a seal for the liberty of Haverford, with the king's arms on one side and two dragons on the other.

No. 541 (m.99), Recorda, Mich.:
Reference to the death of William Rongate, late chamberlain of North Wales, in the Fleet prison.

No. 542 (m.100), *ibid*:
Henry Shirokes is to be attached for the arrears in his account.

No. 543 (m.163d), D.d., Trin.:
Thomas Cheddesworth appoints as his attorneys to account Richard Cheddesworth or Hugh Burghas.

No. 544 (m.209d), Comm., Hil.:
Instructions for the victualling of North Wales castles.

EDWARD III

(as Keeper of the Realm and, after 25 January 1327, as King)

E.368/99   20 Edward II–1 Edward III   (1326–7)

No. 545 (m.8) Comm., Hil.:
Commission to John Stephen and William Sandale to collect the customs at Haverford. (E.159/103, m.8d.) *Latham*, p. 20.

No. 546 (m.9d), *ibid*:
Grant to the men of Carmarthen of various rights for £35 per year. *Latham*, pp. 21–2.

No. 547 (m.61), Fines, Pascha:
Testimony by the controller to Robert Power, chamberlain of North Wales, that the expenditure of £1,180 10s. 4¾d. on works in castles was properly and really incurred. (E.159/103, m.181.) Cf. no. 559. *Latham*, p. 161.

No. 548 (m.66d), D.d., Mich.:
Adjournment allowed for the account of Thomas Esthall, former chamberlain of North Wales. (E.159/103, m.190d.) *Latham*, pp. 172–3.

No. 549 (m.93), Br. Irr., Hil.:
Robert Silkeston is to hand over the records of Glamorgan to William Zouche into whose custody it has been granted through the forfeiture of Hugh Despenser the Younger. (E.159/103, m.147.) *Latham*, p. 223.

No. 550 (mm. 97, 104), Br. Ret., Mich.:
Robert Power, chamberlain of North Wales, is summoned to account. The king is angry that he has failed to appear and will hear no frivolous excuses. Writ (m.104) printed in *Latham*, p. 249. Second writ: the earl of Arundel, justice of Wales, is to bring him.

No. 551 (m.103), *ibid*:
The justice is to distrain the prior of Carmarthen and Thomas Duyn, chamberlain of South Wales, to render account.

No. 552 (103), *ibid*:
Writ to the justice of Wales ordering him to enter the priory of Carmarthen with two loyal men of the town and remove from a chamber there the sum of money deposited there by Thomas Duyn, associated with the prior of Carmarthen, chamberlain of South Wales. Duyn is refusing the prior access to the money, and they are jointly in arrears of £901 17s. 2¼d. Cf. nos. 512, 518, 560. *Latham*, pp. 252–3.

No. 553 (m.108d), *ibid*, Pascha:
Matthew Strange, controller of North Wales under Robert Power, chamberlain, is to come with his rolls.

No. 554 (m.115), Br. Ret., Trin.:
The justice of Wales is to distrain the following:
Rhys ap Gruffydd to account for Llanbadarn castle.
John Langton and Richard Wolf for the lands of the late Hugh Despenser the Younger in Gower.
Robert Singleton, receiver in Gower.
Llywelyn Du ap Gruffydd ap Rhys for Dryslwyn, Dynefawr and all the lands of Cantrefmawr, late of Hugh Despenser the Younger. *Latham*, p. 268.

No. 555 (m.124), St. et Vis., Hil.:
Audit: John Stephen and Robert Cas, customs collectors in Haverford, 29 September 1325 to 13 January 1326. *Latham*, p. 301.

No. 556, *ibid*:
Audit: Robert Clement, keeper of Blaenllyfni and Bwlch Dinas, 14 February 1325 to 10 July 1325. *Latham*, p. 302.

No. 557 (m.124d), *ibid*:
Audit: Robert Morby, keeper of Brecon, late of Humphrey de Bohun, earl of Hereford, 23 January 1325 to 10 July 1326. *Latham*, p. 303.

No. 558 (m.125), *ibid*:
Audit: Thomas Cheddesworth, chamberlain of North Wales, 29 September 1314 to 11 January 1316.
Sum due: £1,058 6s. 9d.
Also owes £1,885 5s. 6½d. of the remainder of his account for the years 29 September 1312 to 29 September 1314.
Combined total due: £2,943 12s. 4d.
After allowances owes £23 1s. 4d. which are to be levied of his benefices in the diocese of Lincoln. (E.159/103, m.216.) Cf. nos. 304, 601. *Latham*, p. 303. Account, S.C.6/1211/7. Enrolled Account, E.372/170, m.55.

No. 559 (m.129), *ibid*, Pascha:
Audit: Robert Power, chamberlain of North Wales, 20 September 1324 to 29 September 1326.
Sum due: £2,839 8s. 11½d. (virtually identical with the total charged in the Enrolled Account, E.372/171, m.40).

After allowances charged with a debt of £632 0s. 10¾d. In October 1327 orders for the levy of this debt from his possessions.
Paid £200 on 5 August 1328 (E.159/103, m.225). Cf. also nos. 547, 651. *Latham*, p. 313.
Counter-roll for 29 September 1325 to 29 September 1326, S.C.6/1213/2. Enrolled Account, E.372/171, m.40.

No. 560 (m.135), *ibid*, Trin.:
Audit: Robert, prior of Carmarthen, and Thomas Duyn, chamberlains of South Wales, 29 September 1321 to 19 September 1325.
Sum due: £1,649 16s. 2½d.
After allowances of payments down to 27 May 1327 owed £913 8s. 1½d. After further allowances, on 27 June 1327 owed £682 17s. 2½d. (cf. no. 518) for which Thomas Duyn was put into the custody of the Marshal of the Exchequer. £210 16s. 4d. were paid up by January 1329, leaving a debt of £472 0s. 10½d. (E.159/103, m.226.) Cf. no. 580. *Latham*, pp. 327–8.
Accounts, S.C.6/1220/1 and 2. Enrolled Account, E.372/171, m.35.

E.159/103   20 Edward II–1 Edward III   (1326–7)

No. 561 m.19), Br. d. Bar., Mich.: the Tower, 1 October 1326:
Licence to Robert Power, chamberlain of North Wales, to account by attorney while he is detained in his bailiwick on the king's business. *Latham*, p. 32.

No. 562 (m.19d), *ibid*: Westminster, 2 October 1326:
Respite of diverse accounts to John Inge, keeper of Wigmore. *Latham*, p. 33.

No. 563 (m.31d), Br. d. Bar., Hil.:
Petition by the villeins of the manor of Penrhos in Anglesey asking to be exonerated of an annual surcharge of £21 7s. 0½d. wrongly levied from them, as they alleged, by reason of unreasonable extent ('irracionabilis extente') of the manor in the time of Edward I. Their request is granted. Cf. nos. 456, 680.

No. 564, *ibid*: Westminster, 3 December 1325:
Quittance to Thomas Cheddesworth, chamberlain of North Wales, of arrears of various annual rents amounting to £12 14s. a year for 6, 7, 8 Edward II. They include:
£3 8s. 6d. excused to the abbot of Bardsey 'pro putura venatorum et canum nostrorum'.
£1 19s. excused to the abbot of Cymmer and also two suits to the courts of Caernarvon and Merioneth.
£3 excused to Llywelyn ap David ap Gruffydd of Edeyrnion for the manor of Crogan.
£1 excused to the free tenants of the commote of Ardudwy in Merioneth 'pro quodam officio quod vocatur Meyryd Kynkellorion' as they allege that they had been deprived of it by the royal bailiffs. *Latham*, p. 44.

No. 565 (m.33d), *ibid*: Westminster, 15 March 1327:
Allowance made to Edmund Dynieton of his expenses in collecting £928 of the subsidy of the Fifteenth granted in 1318 by the men of North Wales for the Scottish War. He said that his expenses amounted to £50 'propter magnam caristiam victualium que tunc erat in partibus predictis'. Cf. no 398. *Latham*, p. 46.

No. 567 (m.45), *ibid*: Westminster, 4 February 1327:
Prior of Pembroke is given livery of his lands which had fallen into the king's hands as an alien house during the recent war against the king of France. *Latham*, p. 54.

No. 568 (m.46d), *ibid*: Westminster, 8 February 1327:
Ditto to the prior of Striguil. *Latham*, p. 54.

No. 569 (m.68d), *ibid*: Westminster, 1 March 1327:
Quittance of a fine imposed on Howel ap Howel. *Latham*, p. 70.

No. 570 (m.92d), *ibid*, Trin.: Westminster, 10 March 1327:
Allowance to Thomas Cheddesworth of £64 19s. 10½d. owed at the Exchequer by Robert Eccleshale, sheriff of Merioneth. He had delivered Eccleshale to Roger Mortimer of Chirk by royal mandate. *Latham*, p. 93.

No. 571 (m.101d), *ibid*: York, 30 June 1327:
Allowances given to Robert Power, chamberlain of North Wales. *Latham*, pp. 102–3.

No. 572 (m.255), Br. Ret., Mich:
Distraint of John Stephen and Robert Cas, customs collectors in Haverford. *Latham*, p. 273.

No. 573 (m.257d), *ibid*:
Distraint of the prior of Carmarthen, sub-collector in St. David's diocese of the Fifteenth of John XXII. *Latham*, p. 277.

No. 574, *ibid*:
Ditto of arrears of £60 7s. 11¾d. out of the arrears of £125 7s. 11¾d. due from him and the prior of Llanthony Prima, collectors of the Tenth of Pope Boniface VIII. *Latham*, p. 277.

No. 575, *ibid*:
Ditto for the arrears of the clerical Moiety of 1294–5, amounting to £35 16s. 11d. *Latham*, p. 277.

No. 576, *ibid*:
The bishop of Llandaff to be similarly distrained for the arrears of the tax of 5d. in the mark. *Latham*, p. 277.

No. 577 (m.259d), *ibid*:
The bishop of Llandaff is to bring to the Exchequer the 1,000m. which he owes the king. *Latham*, p. 281.

E.368/100   2 Edward III   (1327–8)

No. 578 (m.10), Recorda, Mich:
Assignment of the arrears owed by Robert Power, chamberlain of North Wales.

No. 579 (m.19), *ibid*, Hil.:
Deputies of the collectors of the clerical Tenth in the Welsh dioceses named. (E.159/104, m.134.)

No. 580 (mm.28, 29), Recorda, Pascha:
Proceedings concerning the debt of £472 0s. 10½d. owed by Thomas Duyn, one of the chamberlains of South Wales, on his account for the years 29 September 1321 to 19 September 1325 (cf. no. 560). Duyn alleged that the money was in the hands of his various subordinate officials who had been appointed by the late Edmund, earl of Arundel, former justice of Wales, without Duyn's consent, and these officials had failed to give security to Duyn for proper accounting with him (cf. no. 595). The king, by a mandate to the Exchequer of 8 March 1328, ordered that an inquiry be held by the prior of Carmarthen, who was the other chamberlain, together with another person (Robert de Malley being subsequently appointed), into these allegations, and they were empowered to exact all the money in arrears and also to act on their findings to recover these debts. On 21 April 1328, Duyn was granted a respite until the prior of Carmarthen and Malley executed their commission. They certified that, in the years 15–19 Edward II, Edmund, earl of Arundel, and Rhys ap Gruffydd, the earl's lieutenant in South Wales, deputed all officials without consulting Duyn, except for two bedells of Carmarthen and Elfed. They further certified about the names and debts of a long list of officials, with details about the action taken in each case to recover the money. The two commissioners were able to answer, in one way or another, for £391 15s. 8d., out of which they had recovered in cash £130 12s. 1½d. After further proceedings against the debtors and fresh accounting by the Exchequer with Thomas Duyn, he owed in January 1330, of clear debt, £115 9s. 10d., for which he was temporarily committed to the Fleet prison but was later released on mainprise. The debt was still undischarged in 1343 when it was assigned for collection to Edward, prince of Wales, and attempts were again made to exact it in 1349. Cf. also E.159/104, m.70, Br. d. Bar., Pascha.

No. 581 (m.36d), *ibid*:
Matthew Crawthorn attached to account for Neath castle. (E.159/104, m.157d, Trin.)

No. 582 (m.41d), Recorda, Trin.:
Roger Chandos, custodian of Glamorgan, to account for Neath and Caerphilly.

No. 583 (m.47), Fines, Hil.:
Record of expenses on North Wales castles by Thomas Cheddesworth, chamberlain.

No. 584 (m.53d), D.d., Mich.:
After many adjournments a day for account given to Thomas Esthall, chamberlain of North Wales.

No. 585 (m.56d), D.d., Hil.:
The prior of Carmarthen puts in his place to account J. Wynter and Stephen James.

No. 586 (m.63d), D.d., Pascha:
Llywelyn Du ap Gruffydd ap Rhys puts in his place to account John, clerk of Carmarthen for Cantrefmawr, and the issues of the castles of Dryslwyn and Dynefwr, late of Hugh Despenser the Younger.

No. 587 (m.75), Br. Ret., Mich:
Mandate to Robert Power to render account. Cf. also *infra*, m.83 (order to distrain him).

No. 588 (m.75d), *ibid*:
Roger Mortimer ordered to render account for Wigmore.

No. 589, *ibid*:
Roger Chandos ordered to render account for Glamorgan.

No. 590 (m.77d), *ibid*:
Thomas Cheddesworth is to be given allowances in his account for 29 September 1314 to 9 January 1315 for money spent on repairs to Caernarvon, Criccieth and Beaumaris. (E.159/104, m.50d, and also m.78d.)

No. 591 (m.92), St. et Vis., Mich.:
Allowance in the account of the sheriff of Lincoln for a pension of £20 a year paid to Gwenllian, daughter of Llywelyn, late prince of Wales, nun of Sempringham.

No. 592 (m.93d), *ibid*:
Audit of the account of John Stonore of Haverford, and William Sandale, collectors of the wool custom at Haverford.

No. 593 (m.97d), *ibid*, Hil.:
Audit: Robert, prior of Carmarthen, and Thomas Duyn, associated with him, chamberlains of South Wales, 29 September 1325 to 29 September 1326. Sum due: £342 13s. 1½d.
Allowances include £259 2s. 8d. for wages, during eight days, of men-at-arms and infantry conducted by Rhys ap Gruffydd to Brecon towards King Edward II. They were raised and led to the king in pursuance of a mandate under the privy seal of Edward II, dated at Gloucester on 11 October 1326, ordering Rhys to proceed to the king with utmost haste with such men-at-arms, hobelars and infantry as he could possibly gather to serve at the king's wages.
After allowances they owe £63 10s. 10½d.

E.159/104 2 Edward III (1327–8)

No. 594 (m.31), Br. d. Bar., Hil.: York, 20 January 1328:
The bishop of Bangor pleads that he was not, in the time of the princes of Wales, held liable for escaped prisoners, and that Edward I had confirmed this. Endorsed that it is confirmed again by royal letters patent.

No. 595 (m.70), *ibid*, Pascha: York, 8 March 1328:
It has been shown by Thomas Duyn, late chamberlain of South Wales, that Edmund, earl of Arundel, late justice of Wales, appointed officials without his consent, who then fell into arrears with which the chamberlain was charged. He was also unjustly charged with the revenues of lands which were actually in the hands of the justice because Thomas had been an adherent of the earl of Lancaster. Cf. no. 580.

No. 596 (m.80), *ibid*, Trin.: York, 2 March 1328:
Custody of Denbigh castle granted to Roger Mortimer of Wigmore.

No. 597 (m.83d), *ibid*: Northampton, 17 May 1328:
Acquittance to Thomas Cheddesworth, chamberlain of North Wales, for discharging an assignment on his revenues, by paying Hugh Audley for horses lost in the king's service.

No. 598 (m.95d), *ibid*: Northampton, 6 May 1328:
The Abbot of Tintern is made quit of various rents.

No. 599 (m.115), Communia, Mich.:
Acquittance given to William de la Bataille, clerk of Robert Power, chamberlain of North Wales.

No. 600 (m.149), Recorda, Pascha:
The prior of Carmarthen is to enquire concerning money owed by Thomas Duyn, who is in the Fleet prison.

No. 601 (m.168), St. et Vis., Mich.:
View: Thomas Cheddesworth, chamberlain of North Wales, for expenditure on Welsh castles in 1314–15.
Accounted for £1,494 4s. 6d., spent at Caernarvon, Beaumaris, Conway and Criccieth. Cf. nos. 583, 590.

No. 602 (m.233d), Br. Irr., Hil.:
Allowance to be made to the chamberlain of South Wales for money owed to Roger Swynerton for soldiers for the Scottish war, 1327.

No. 603 (m.234), *ibid*:
Rhys ap Howel had found defects in Dynefwr castle. Mandate to Edmund Hakelut, now constable, to repair these.

No. 604 (m.239), *ibid*, Trin.:
Assignment of the proceeds of the clerical Tenth in Llandaff diocese to the Bardi of Florence, to be paid by the abbot of Tintern, its collector.

No. 605 (m.240), Br. Ret., Mich.:
The prior of Carmarthen and Thomas Duyn are to pay such revenues as they have to Arnald Micol, a royal creditor.

No. 606 (m.244), *ibid*:
Demand of arrears from John Stephen and Robert Cas, customs collectors at Haverford.

No. 607 (m.247d), *ibid*, Hil.:
The debts due to Hugh Despenser in Wales are to be paid to the executors of John Hastings in recompense for lands appropriated by the Despensers.

No. 608 (m.250d), *ibid*:
The justice of Wales is to repair the walls of Conway in reply to a petition of the burgesses.

E.368/101   3 Edward III   (1328–9)

No. 609 (m.8), Comm., Pascha:
Commission to John Stephen of Haverford and William Sandale to collect the customs. (E.159/105, m.8.)

No. 610 (m.8d), *ibid*:
Instructions to John Paynel, chamberlain of Chester, to sell the victuals in the castles of Chester, Flint, Rhuddlan and Beeston as they may have deteriorated and cannot be saved. Cf. *infra*, m.44. He is to render account for money received from the sale.

No. 611 (m.42), Recorda, Pascha:
Confirmation of the grant of 'Huwaldesfeld' to the abbot of Tintern.

No. 612 (m.49), *ibid*, Trin.:
The king wishes to be informed of the case brought against Thomas Duyn. (E.159/105, Br. d. Bar., Trin., m.80; Recogn., Trin., m.167.)

No. 613 (mm.72d, 73d), D.d., Hil.:
A day for account is given to Robert Power, late chamberlain of North Wales.

No. 614 (m.80d), *ibid*, Pascha:
A day for account is given to Adam Wetenhale, late chamberlain of North Wales.

No. 615 (m.83), D.d., Trin.:
John Seymour, merchant, put in his place to account Ben' le Bray or John Veys against Thomas Duyn, late chamberlain of South Wales, for wine lately taken into the port of Carmarthen.

No. 616 (m.84), *ibid*:
John Seymour put in his place John Witsand, citizen of London, against Thomas Duyn for wine taken to the port of Carmarthen.

No. 617 (m.95), Br. Irr., Mich.:
Allowance to the prior of Carmarthen, chamberlain of South Wales, in his account for money assigned to Arnald Micol. (E.159/105, m.242, Br. Irr., Mich.)

No. 618 (m.101), Br. Ret., Mich.:
Threats of action against the prior of Carmarthen, chamberlain of South Wales, if he fails to come to account.

No. 619 (m.102), *ibid*:
William Chisenhale, custodian of the victuals in Caerphilly castle, is to sell them quickly and come to account. (E.159/105, m.198d, D.d., Hil.)

No. 620 (m.112), *ibid*, Pascha:
John Chiversdon, late chamberlain of North Wales, is to be distrained for failure to account.

No. 621 (m.119d), St. et Vis., Mich.:
Audit to the account of John Stephen of Haverford and William Sandale, collectors of the Ancient Custom at Haverfordwest, 29 September 1327 to 29 September 1328.

No. 622 (m.132), *ibid*, Trin.:
View: prior of Cardigan, collector of the clerical Tenth in the archdeaconry of Cardigan.
Sum due: £48 os. 10d.
Paid £40 and owes £8 os. 10d.

No. 622a (m.133d), *ibid*:
View: abbot of Conway, collector of the clerical Tenth in the diocese of St. Asaph.
Sum due: £127.
Paid £120 and owes £7.

No. 623, *ibid*:
Audit: dean and chapter of Bangor, collectors of the clerical Tenth in that diocese.
Sum due: £5 2s. 7d.
After allowances they owe £1 14s. 7d.

E.159/105   3 Edward III   (1328–9)

No. 624 (mm.35, 36), Br. d. Bar.: Gloucester, 3 October 1328:
Grant of £20 to Gwenllian, nun of Sempringham, daughter of Llywelyn, late prince of Wales.

No. 625 (m.35d), *ibid*: York, 8 August 1328:
The prior of Carmarthen not to be charged with the clerical Tenth of Pope Boniface VIII in the reign of Edward I.

No. 626 (m.53), *ibid*: Westminster, 9 February 1329:
Allowance in his account given to Thomas Cheddesworth, late chamberlain of North Wales, for animals brought to England and sent to Windsor.

No. 627 (m.53d), *ibid*: Eltham, 29 February 1329:
Allowance in his account for the same chamberlain for the expenses of ships for John Ergal, going from Aberconway to Scotland and Ireland. Cf. also E.368/102, m.17d, Recorda, Mich. (E.159/106, Recorda, Mich., m.15od.)

No. 628 (m.54), *ibid*.: Eltham, 29 February 1329:
Thomas Cheddesworth, late chamberlain of North Wales, sought the payment of the fee of 40m. which had been due to him and which the Exchequer had not paid.

No. 629 (m.90d), *ibid*, Trin.: Guildford, 6 July 1329:
Money unduly exacted from Henry Shirokes, late chamberlain of North Wales, as debt, is to be restored to him.

No. 630 (m.178d), D.d., Trin.:
Isabella, the king's mother, puts in her place to account for the issues of her lands in Wales, John Oxendon.

No. 631 (m.198d), D.d., Hil.:
A day for account is given to Thomas Esthall, late chamberlain of North Wales, and William Chisenhale, late custodian of goods in Caerphilly castle.

No. 632 (m.224), St. et Vis., Trin.:
View: prior of Cardigan, collector of the clerical Tenth, diocese of St. David's.
Sum due: £48 os. 1od.
After payment of £40 owes £8 os. 1od.

No. 633 (m.243), Br. Irr., Mich.:
Assignment to merchants of the clerical Tenth (St. David's diocese) collected by the priors of Blakeney, Pembroke, Cardigan and Kidwelly.

No. 634 (m.244), *ibid*, Hil.:
Instructions to the constable to use some of the revenue of Dryslwyn castle for the repair of the castle.

No. 635 (m.250d), Br. Ret., Mich.:
The justice of Wales is to distrain the abbot of Valle Crucis, collector of Pope Boniface's clerical Tenth, St. Asaph diocese. (E.159/106, m.293d.)

E.368/102   4 Edward III   (1329–30)

No. 636 (m.12d), Recorda, Mich.:
The justice of Wales is to enquire what were the goods of John Chiveresdon, chamberlain of North Wales, who died in office. (E.159/106, m.146d.)

No. 637 (m.17), *ibid*:
Writ to Roger Mortimer, justice of Wales, to bring Robert Power, late chamberlain, and his controllers, to account for the year 1326–7.

No. 638 (m.72d), Fines, Mich.:
Matthew le Strange, lieutenant successively of Edmund, earl of Arundel, Richard Damory and Roger Mortimer (of Wigmore), justices of all Wales, is to come with his counter-rolls to the Exchequer to certify it about the allowances that should be made to Robert Power in his account as former chamberlain of North Wales. (E.159/106, m.221d; cf. also m.150, Recorda, Mich.) Cf. nos. 496, 547, 559, 651.

No. 639 (m.82d), *ibid*:
Robert Power, former chamberlain of North Wales, placed William de la Bataille in his place when he went to Ireland. (E.159/106, m.32d, Br. d. Bar., Mich.)

No. 640 (m.87), D.d., Mich.:
A day for account is given to Thomas Esthall and Robert Power, late chamberlains of North Wales. (E.159/106, m.243, D.d., Mich.)

No. 641 (m.93d), D.d., Pascha:
A day for account is given to Nicholas Acton, parson of Wystaneston, chamberlain of North Wales. (E.159/106, m.246d.)

No. 642 (m.108), Recogn., Pascha:
William Menillo, prior of Pembroke, recognised that he owed the prior of the Friars Preachers at Oxford £16 12s. 5¾d. (E.159/106, m.112.) Cf. no. 653.

No. 643 (m.114), Br. Irr., Hil.:
Mandate to the prior of Carmarthen, chamberlain of South Wales, to pay the bishop of St. David's £60 for his mission to France in the king's service.

No. 644 (m.117d), *ibid*:
Mandate to Roger Mortimer, justice of Wales, and Nicholas Acton, chamberlain of North Wales, to enquire into the goods of the late John Chiveresdon, chamberlain of North Wales.

No. 645 (m.121), Br. Ret., Mich.:
The justice of Wales is to distrain the dean and chapter of Bangor, collectors of the clerical Tenth in the diocese of Bangor (1327).

No. 646 (m.123), *ibid*:
The prior of Carmarthen and Thomas Duyn are to be distrained for the arrears of their account for the chamberlainship of South Wales.

No. 647 (m.136), *ibid*, Trin.:
The bishop of St. David's is to distrain Thomas Duyn as he is beneficed in that diocese.

No. 648 (m.137), St. et Vis., Mich.:
Audit: prior of Cardigan, collector of the clerical Tenth in the archdeaconry of Cardigan.
Sum due: £8 os. 10d.
After allowance of £3 6s. 8d. for his expenses, he owes £4 14s. 2d.

No. 649 (m.137d), *ibid*:
Audit: abbot of Conway, collector of the clerical Tenth in the diocese of St. Asaph.
Sum due: £4 12s 3d.
Paid £4 12s. and owes 3d.

No. 650 (m.138), *ibid*:
Audit: abbot of Tintern, collector of the clerical Tenth in the diocese of Llandaff.
Sum due: £7 os. o¾d.
Paid 7s. 10d. and owes £6 12s. 2¾d.

No. 651 (m.143), St. et Vis., Mich.:
Audit: Robert Power, chamberlain of North Wales, 29 September 1326 to 31 October 1327.
Sum due: £1,353 5s. 9½d.
After allowances owed £932 16s. 5d. and also £2,839 8s. 11½d. of the arrears of previous accounts (cf. no. 559).
Joint debt: £3,771 19s. 4½d.
After allowances owed £2 os. 6¼d.
Enrolled Account, E.372/173, m.45.

No. 652 (m.148d), *ibid*, Hil.:
Audit: Thomas Esthall, chamberlain of North Wales.
Sum due: £9,858 consisting of:
(i) £1,350 5s. 5½d. of the remainder of the account of 29 September 1302 to 29 September 1305.
Account, *B.B.C.S.* 1 (1922), pp. 257–75.
(ii) £2,338 10s. 2d. for the years 29 September 1305 to 29 September 1307. Originally charged with £2,701 2s., but this was reduced through provisional allowances.
Account *B.B.C.S.* 16 (1955), pp. 111–33.

(iii) £6,169 4s. 3½d. for the years 29 September 1307 to 29 September 1312. Committed to the Fleet prison on 10 March 1330, and in the Trinity term 1330 committed to the Tower of London. Freed by mainprise in the Easter term 1331. Cf. nos. 303, 356, 377, 681-4.
Accounts, S.C.6/1211/2a, 2b, 4, 5. Enrolled Account, E.372/176, mm.53, 54.

No. 653 (m.157), *ibid*, Pascha:
Audit: prior of St. Nicholas, Pembroke, collector of the clerical Tenth, St. David's diocese.
Sum due: £20 12s 5¾d.
After allowances owed £16 12s. 5¾d. which were assigned on 23 May 1330 to the Dominican convent at Oxford. Cf. no. 642.

E.159/106   4 Edward III   (1329-30)

No. 654 (m.17), Br. d. Bar., Mich.: Worcester, 3 October 1329:
The Exchequer is to ascertain if sufficient allowances were made to Thomas Esthall in his account. Cf. nos. 652, 681-4.

No. 655 (m.20), *ibid*: Worcester, 8 October 1329:
The Exchequer is to enquire whether the manor of Accleston (Herefordshire) is held by the bishop of Llandaff as a temporality. (E.159/107, Br. d. Bar., Pascha.) Cf. no. 822.

No. 656 (m.23d), *ibid*: Dunstable, 20 October 1329:
60m. granted to Guillo ap Lethyn for service to King Edward II.

No. 657 (m.44), *ibid*, Hil.: Kenilworth, 22 December 1329:
Plea by the bishop of Llandaff not to be forced to pay debts exacted by the late Hugh Despenser to the new lord of Newburgh, Hugh Audley.

No. 658 (m.59d), *ibid*: Eltham, 10 February 1330:
The custody of all the lands of John Giffard of Brimpsfield in Wales as well as in England is given to John Mautravers, junior.

No. 659 (m.71), *ibid*, Pascha: Winchester, 16 March 1330:
Edward II, before he became king, as prince of Wales committed various offices, castles, manors, and also bishoprics, abbeys and other vacant religious houses to custodians to answer to him in his Chamber or in other ways. He did so by instruments under his Privy Seal. These people never accounted or else, if they had accounted, never answered for the arrears due. Orders to ascertain who held these commissions so that the accounts could be pursued as required. The king has ordered any who were keepers of the Privy Seal of his father to certify him concerning these commissions.

No. 660 (m.229d), D.d., Mich.:
The abbot of Tintern puts in his place Gilbert of Stowe, fellow monk, to account for the clerical Tenth in the diocese of Llandaff.

No. 661 (m.240d), *ibid*:
Respite of account for the prior of Carmarthen, chamberlain of South Wales, at the instance of Roger Mortimer of Wigmore.

No. 662 (m.244d), *ibid*, Hil.:
A day is given to Llywelyn Du ap Gruffydd ap Rhys to account for Dryslwyn, Dynefawr and Cantrefmawr.

No. 663 (m.249), *ibid*, Trin.:
The prior of Brecon, collector of the clerical Tenth in the archdeaconry of Brecon, puts in his place to account Elias Waddesworth, clerk, or Adam Vavasour, to render account.

No. 664 (m.296d), Br. Ret., Mich.:
The executors of the bishop of Llandaff, collector of the tax of five pence in the mark in Llandaff diocese, are to be distrained.

E.368/103   5 Edward III   (1330–1)

No. 665 (m.15d), Recorda, Mich.:
Bestowal by Thomas Beauchamp, earl of Warwick, of the office of the chamberlain of the Exchequer (at Westminster) on Nicholas Acton (formerly chamberlain of North Wales until 14 August 1330; cf. no. 680).

No. 666 (m.71), *ibid*:
Exoneration from debt of the collectors of the Fifteenth in Flint (under Edward I), Patrick Haselwell and Robert Pulle.

No. 667 (m.91), D.d., Mich.:
Llywelyn Du ap Gruffydd ap Rhys puts in his place John de la Brock in proceedings against the chamberlain of South Wales to account for £4 owed as constable of Mathlaen in Cantrefmawr. Cf. also m.16d, Recorda, Mich. (E.159/107, Recorda, Hil.)

No. 668 (m.91d), *ibid*:
A day for account is given to Nicholas Acton, chamberlain of North Wales.

No. 669 (m.109), *ibid*, Trin.:
A day for accounting for the goods in North Wales castles is given to Robert Power. He puts William de la Bataille as his attorney.

No. 670 (m.126d), Br. Irr., Hil.:
£300 out of the issues of the chamberlainship of South Wales is to be paid to Queen Philippa for the expenses of her household.

No. 671 (m.127d), *ibid*, Trin.:
Allowance is given in his account to the prior of Carmarthen, chamberlain of South Wales, for payments made to John Estre, as the king owes debts to Estre for payments made in Essex and Hertfordshire.

No. 672 (m.128), Br. Ret., Mich.:
Mandate to the justice of Wales to distrain Alexandra St. John for marrying illegally John, son and heir of Hugh Luckombe.

No. 673 (m.134), *ibid*:
Order to distrain for arrears the dean and chapter of Bangor, collectors of the clerical Tenth, Bangor diocese. (1 Edward III.)

No. 674 (m.134d), *ibid*, Hil.:
The heir of Gruffydd ap Gwenwynwyn is to be distrained to pay a relief.

No. 675 (m.136), *ibid*:
Order to distrain William Shalford, controller, to provide the counter-rolls so that Nicholas Acton, chamberlain of North Wales, can conclude his account.

No. 676 (m.139d), Br. Ret., Hil.:
Writ to the prior of Carmarthen, chamberlain of South Wales, to send to the king all the ready money he has in his possession.

No. 677 (m.140d), *ibid*:
Richard Simon is to be distrained to produce the issues of Castle Martin, Pembroke, 'Lyngeswoode', Tenby and Haverford.

No. 678 (m.146d), *ibid*, Trin.:
The prior of Carmarthen to be distrained by the justice of Wales.

No. 679 (m.153d), *ibid*:
Robert Power, chamberlain of North Wales, requests quittance from responsibility for arrears owed by his deputies, Anian ap Ieuan, sheriff of Anglesey, Madog Gloth and Henry Somery, late sub-sheriffs, and Griffin ap Rhys, late sheriff of Merioneth. Although he has put them in gaol they still fail to account with him.

No. 680 (m.171d), St. et Vis., Pascha:
Audit: Nicholas Acton, chamberlain of North Wales, 20 March 1329 to 14 August 1330.
Sum due: £2,161 0s. 7¼d.
Among allowances claims £21 7s. 0½d. a year's surcharge of rent of the villeins of the manor of Penrhos in Anglesey which, in the extent made after the conquest of Wales by Edward I, was, through error, so surcharged, and the sum could never be collected after this extent was applied, as was allowed in the account of Robert Power, former chamberlain, enrolled in E.372/169, m.46d. Cf. nos. 456, 563.
After allowance has a surplus of £1 19s. 1½d. (E.159/107, St. et Vis., Pascha.)
Enrolled Account, E.372/175, m.50.

No. 681 (mm.186r, 186d), *ibid*, Trin.:

Audit: Thomas Esthall, chamberlain of North Wales, 29 September 1302 to 29 September 1312.

Sum due: £10,220 11s. 10d. consisting of:

(i) £1,350 5s. 5½d. of the remainder of his account, 29 September 1302 to 29 September 1305. Account, *B.B.C.S.* 1 (1922), pp. 257-75.

(ii) £2,701 2s. for the years 29 September 1305 to 29 September 1307. Account, *B.B.C.S.* 16 (1955), pp. 111-33.

(iii) £6,169 4s. 4½d. for the years 29 September 1307 to 29 September 1312. Paid £401 7s. 1d. in June–July 1331.

Claims for allowance provisionally accepted: £5,784 3s. 6½d. Include payments for 300 infantry sent from North Wales to Carlisle in 34 Edward I for service against the Scots, led by Gruffydd ap Rhys, knight; 950 infantry sent from North Wales in October 1309 to serve against the Scots.

2,000 infantry selected in August 1310 for service against the Scots. In 1310 they were selected by Gruffudd Thloyt, Hugh Venables, Richard Poulesden and Yereward ap Gruffudd.

After these payments and allowances remained a debt of £4,093 18s. 2½d., adjourned for further consideration. (E.159/107, St. et Vis., Pascha.)

Royal letter of allowance on behalf of Esthall of 3 October 1329 in *B.B.C.S.* 16 (1955), p. 111.

Cf. nos. 303, 356, 377, 652, 682-4.

Enrolled Account, E.372/176, mm.53, 54, 55.

No. 682 (mm.187r, 187d), *ibid*:

Schedule of petitions of Thomas Esthall, chamberlain of North Wales, listing items for which he claimed allowance, totalling £4,300 9s. 7d. They included further details about items considered in no. 681.

Claims included £86 13s. 4d. of the value of Esthall's lands which had been in the king's hands for the previous twenty years, being valued at £4 6s. 8d. a year.

No. 683 (mm.188r, 188d), *ibid*:

Schedule of claims for allowance submitted by Thomas Esthall, chamberlain of North Wales, for expenditure on castles, totalling £2,040 13s. 3¾d. Cf. no. 681.

No. 684 (m.189), *ibid*:

Resumption of audit of Thomas Esthall, chamberlain of North Wales. Debt still under consideration: £4,093 18s. 2½d. (cf. no. 681).

Allowance could not be granted previously for £2,040 13s. 3¾d. (cf. no. 683) because of the destruction in a fire of the counter-rolls of Hugh Audley the Elder, former justice of Wales. They were burnt at his manor of Arle long before his death (*ob. c.* 1325). Their destruction attested in a letter of Audley in the custody of the Exchequer which the king ordered the Exchequer to allow by his mandate of 15 October 1331, by virtue of which Esthall was allowed to proceed to his final account on 4 December 1331.

After further allowances owes £1,690 15s. o¾d. pardoned to him by a royal mandate enrolled on the memoranda roll of 6 Edward III. (Two pardons to Esthall of 13 and 20 November 1331, *C.P.R.*, 1330–4, pp. 219, 222). Enrolled Account, E.372/176, m.354.

E.159/107   5 Edward III   (1330–1)

No. 685 (m.73), Br. d. Bar., Hil.: Privy Seal, Westminster, 21 January 1331: Allowance is to be made in his account to Roger Northburgh, bishop of Chester, for the expenses incurred in seizing Caerphilly castle into the king's hands. Cf. also Recorda, Trin.

No. 686, *ibid*: Hertford, 20 January 1331: The bishop of St. David's pleaded that he owned nothing in the town of Great Stanmore (archdeaconry of Middlesex) and should not be taxed there.

No. 687 (mm.114 and 115), *ibid*, Pascha: Wingham, 22 April 1331: The Exchequer is to speed up the final accounting of Robert Power, chamberlain of North Wales, as he is going overseas.

No. 688 (m.117d), *ibid*: Havering atte Boure, 8 May 1331: Henry Shirokes seeks allowances at the Exchequer in consideration of the failure of some of his deputies to account.

No. 689 (m.118), *ibid*: Havering atte Boure, 5 May 1331; and four writs dated Dartford, 4 May 1331: Five writs concerning the account of Robert Power, chamberlain of North Wales.

No. 690 (m.123), *ibid*, Trin.: Privy Seal, Clipston, 23 September 1330: A sum of £200 paid by Nicholas Acton to Roger Mortimer on the verbal order of the king is to be allowed in his account as chamberlain of North Wales.

No. 691 (m.124d), *ibid*: Privy Seal, Norwich, 8 June 1331: The king wants to know the issues of the vills of 'Clenyok, Lanlibyon, Geyru and Kelgwyn' in Anglesey.

No. 692 (m.126), *ibid*: Allowance is to be made to Nicholas Acton, chamberlain of North Wales, for £48 10s. 5d. owed to him by Edward I for service at Berwick on Tweed. Westminster, 15 December 1330.

No. 693, *ibid*: Bury St. Edmunds, 8 June 1331: Gift of £300 made to Robert Power, former chamberlain of North Wales, in recompense for the expenses incurred by him in assuring the safe-keeping of North Wales at the time of the pursuing of Hugh Despenser and certain other enemies of the king. His services have been attested by many magnates of the king's council.

No. 694 (m.171), Recorda, Hil.:
Memorandum that Thomas Hampton, Steward of Roger Mortimer (of Wigmore) in Pembroke, which was in the king's custody through the minority of Laurence Hastings, handed in a document containing certain grants made by Roger Mortimer in England.

No. 695 (m.171d), *ibid*:
Llywelyn Du ap Gruffydd ap Rhys, steward of Cantrefmawr, Dryslwyn and Dynefwr, formerly the property of Hugh Despenser the Younger, is to account.

No. 696 (m.249), Fines, Pascha:
Manucaption for Thomas Esthall, late chamberlain of North Wales.

No. 697 (m.268), D.d., Mich.:
The prior of Carmarthen put in his place Stephen James and John his clerk to render account.

No. 698 (m.284), *ibid*, Trin.:
A day is given for account for the goods of North Wales castles delivered to Robert Power, chamberlain.

No. 699 (m.333d), B. Irr., Hil.:
2s. 10d. a day expenses for coming to Westminster granted to William Werdale, Richard Suthorp and Robert Perrers, supervisors of the castles and goods of the late Roger Mortimer, earl of March.

No. 700 (m.338d), *ibid*, Trin.:
Allowances in his account made to Adam Withiford, late chamberlain of North Wales, for money paid to Arnald Micol, merchant.

No. 701, *ibid*:
The same to Robert Hambury, late chamberlain.

No. 702 (m.343), Br. Ret., Mich.:
The abbot of Valle Crucis, late sub-collector of the clerical Tenth, to be distrained for arrears.

No. 703 (m.343d), *ibid*:
The priors of Brecon and Kidwelly to be similarly distrained.

No. 704 (m.350), *ibid*, Hil.:
William Creppings is to reply to the king for debts owed to the late Roger Mortimer, earl of March. (E.159/108, mm.236, 237, Recorda, Trin.)

No. 705 (m.350d), *ibid*:
Robert Perrers, late custodian of Haverfordwest, and Richard Baytson, late custodian of Denbigh, are to be brought to account.

No. 706, *ibid*, Pascha:

The justice of Wales is to reply for the goods taken by the following: William Helpeston, Philip Lawr, William Tonkare of Henllys (£200); Skirewith le Traventer of Cardiff (£10); Philip Res (£10); Rhys Du (£400); William le Hunt (£20); John Langeton (£300); Robert Maunxel (30s.); Hamo Turbervill (£20); John ap Walter Vaughan (£20); David ap Walter Vaughan (£20); William ap Walter Vaughan (£20); Richard le Wolf (£100); Robert de la Mare (£10); John Testard, senior (108s. 3d.); Richard Welles (£300); Robert Perciebrigg (£25); John Philip (5s.); Philip Res, John Horton, Henry Ditton (£10); Robert Careman (20s.); William le Porteur, Adam le Corour and Henry Durant (£40); John Penres (£20); Richard Penres (20s.); Richard Scorlag (40s.); Richard Maunxel (15s.), Howel ap Thomas (£20), Ieuan ap Eynon and John his brother (100s.); Eynon Vychan and Howel his son (100s.); Morgan ap Meurig (£40); Thomas Blew (100s.); Walter Bexe, Roger Basingho, John Dun, Bernard Dun, Robert Dun, Richard Wadekyn, William Legat, Roger Chaundler, Cadwgan ap Gruffydd, William and Gruffydd his brothers, William ap Cadwgan Ieuan ap Goulhaved and his five sons for goods worth £1,000; Walter le Wise (5m.), Cutwyn ap Philip (12s. 4d.).

These goods, which were held by the king, our father (Edward II at the time of his capture by Mortimer) at Swansea were taken away by these people. By inquisition of Richard Peshale and David de la Bere, 23 April 1331.

E.368/104   6 Edward III   (1331–2)

No. 707 (m.9), Comm., Hil.:

The prior of Carmarthen, chamberlain of South Wales, is to be distrained.

No. 708, *ibid*:

Thomas Clonne, custodian of Cefnllys and of the lands of the late Roger Mortimer of Chirk, failed to produce an extent of the lands of Maelienydd, Dolforwyn and Cydewain, and is summoned to the Exchequer. (E.159/108, m.230, Recorda, Pascha, put in Fleet prison.)

No. 709 (m.54), Recorda, Trin.:

John Dene to come to account for the castles and lands of Bwlchdinas, Blaenllyfni and Pencelly, and the goods of the late Roger Mortimer of Chirk there.

No. 710 (m.57d), D.d., Mich.:

All goods of Robert Hambury, chamberlain of North Wales, are to pass into the king's hands after many failures to account, and he is put in the Fleet prison.

No. 711 (m.78d), *ibid*:

Robert Power puts as his attorneys William Peck, William Power and John Eneffeld in an action against Anian ap Ieuan, late sheriff of Anglesey, for arrears. (E.159/108, m.297d.)

No. 712 (m.97), *ibid*, Hil.:
Robert Perrers, custodian of Haverfordwest, puts in his place to account Robert Martyn and John de Villa Arnold'. (E.159/108, m.300.)

No. 713 (m.118d), Br. Irr., Pascha:
The chamberlain of South Wales is ordered to pay Thomas Blaunkfront £40 p.a. out of the issues of Emlyn castle.

No. 714 (m.119d), *ibid*, Trin.:
Richard Simond, steward of Pembroke and custodian of royal castles, is assigned to pay Bartholomew Thomasyn, merchant, £50.

No. 715 (m.125d), Br. Ret., Mich.:
The bishop of Llandaff is instructed to distrain the abbot of Tintern for arrears of the clerical Tenth, of £6 12s. 2¼d. (1326–7).

No. 716 (m.128d), *ibid*:
Writ of distraint against Thomas Duyn, chamberlain of South Wales, wherever he is beneficed.

No. 717 (m.128), *ibid*:
Writ of distraint against prior of Carmarthen for 40s. of the goods of his colleague Thomas Duyn, chamberlain of South Wales.

No. 718 (m.134), *ibid*:
Writ summoning the prior of Carmarthen to account. Cf. also *infra*, m.144d, Br. Ret., Pascha.

No. 719 (m.136), Br. Ret., Hil.:
The following to be distrained to account:
  John Benet for Monmouth,
  John Langton, Richard Wolf and Robert Singleton for Gower, late of Hugh Despenser the Younger,
  Llewelyn Du ap Gruffydd ap Rhys for Dryslwyn, Dynefwr and Cantref-mawr, late of Hugh Despenser the Younger.

No. 720 (m.138), *ibid*:
Robert Hambury, late chamberlain of North Wales, to be distrained.

No. 721 (m.139d), *ibid*:
The men of Chirk are to be distrained for the money owed for the confirmation of their charter.

No. 722 (m.148d), Br. Ret., Trin.:
Distraint of the prior of Carmarthen. (E.159/108, m.11, Comm., Hil.)

No. 723 (m.159), St. et Vis., Mich.:
Audit: Robert Power, chamberlain of North Wales, for goods and equipment received in the Welsh castles from the outgoing chamberlain, Adam Wetenhale, at Easter 1323.
Sum due: £107 4s. 6½d. for which he accounted satisfactorily.
Power was exonerated of a further sum of £174 11s. 3½d., for which Anian ap Ieuan, sheriff of Anglesey, was committed to Fleet prison.
(E. 159/108, m.310.) Enrolled Account, E.372/176, m.61.

No. 724 (m.160), *ibid*:
Audit: Nicholas Acton, chamberlain of North Wales, for stores at castles there, 18 April 1329 to 14 August 1330.
Sum due: £7 19s. 10d.
Allowed in his surplus in his main Enrolled Account, E.372/175, m.50.
Enrolled Account for stores, E.372/176, m.66.

E.159/108   6 Edward III   (1331–2)

No. 725 (m.33), Br. d. Bar., Mich.: Westminster, 12 December 1331:
The chamberlain of Chester is to see that the inhabitants of Rhuddlan mend the bridge which is in a dangerous condition.

No. 726 (m.51d), *ibid*: Westminster, 15 October 1331:
Allowance to Thomas Esthall, chamberlain of North Wales, for money paid into the Wardrobe in the time of Edward II. Cf. nos. 681–4.

No. 727 (m.52), *ibid*: Westminster, 12 October 1331:
Allowance made to the same Thomas Esthall for money due from him beyond his fee for which, in ignorance, he had failed to make account. Cf. nos. 681–4.

No. 728 (m.53), *ibid*: Westminster, 15 October 1331:
Allowance to Esthall for expenses on North Wales castles although the destruction of the counter-rolls and death of controller makes proper account impossible. Cf. nos. 681–4.

No. 729 (m.54d), *ibid*: Westminster, 15 October 1331:
Record that the above-mentioned counter-rolls were burnt accidentally at Hothefield. Cf. also *infra*, m.66. Cf. nos. 681–4.

No. 730 (m.55), *ibid*: Westminster, October 1331:
Record concerning a plea by Richard, earl of Arundel, about a debt owed by his father, the late Edmund, earl of Arundel, to the late Roger Mortimer.

No. 731 (mm.60r and d), *ibid*: Marlborough, 8 November 1331:
Long list of allowances to Thomas Esthall. Cf. nos. 681–4.

No. 732 (m.63), *ibid*: Guildford, 20 November 1331:
Examination is to be made to see if allowances claimed by Robert Power, chamberlain of North Wales, to Anian ap Ieuan, sheriff of Anglesey, are correct.

No. 733 (m.133d), *ibid*, Pascha: Woodstock, 26 May 1332:
The Exchequer is to discover how much is owed to Cynfrig Sais ap David and William ap Howel ap 'Kedivor', bedells of the commote of Mefenydd.

No. 734 (m.137), *ibid*: Barnwell, 6 May 1332:
A petition in parliament by the prior of Llanthony is sent to the Exchequer where the endorsement is to be acted upon.

No. 735 (m.164), Recorda, Trin.:
William Shalford of Caernarvon and Anian ap Ieuan of Anglesey recognise that they owe Isabella, Queen of England, £340 for the manors of 'Roffei, Dolbenmaen, Penmaghan' and the commote of Menai demised to them.

No. 736 (m.265), Fines, Trin.:
Manucaption for John Esseby who has failed to account for Englefield.

No. 737 (m.355), Br. Irr., Hil.:
Assignment of £500 each from the issues of the chamberlainship of North and South Wales to the Bardi of Florence.

No. 738 (m.355d), *ibid*:
Richard Symond, farmer of the manor of Pembroke, to pay £200 to Anthony Bache of Genoa.

E.368/105   7 Edward III   (1332–3)

No. 739 (m.13), Recorda, Mich.:
Allowance to Robert Hambury for the issues of Anglesey for which he cannot make account. (E.159/109, m.109.)

No. 740 (m.22), *ibid*:
Inquisition is to be made on the goods of the late Thomas Chiveresdon, late chamberlain of North Wales. (E.159/109, m.117.)

No. 741 (m.41), Recorda, Pascha:
Thomas Clonne, late custodian of Cefnllys and other lands of the late Roger Mortimer is put in the Fleet prison. (E.159/109, m.155.) *Infra*, m.51, Fines, Mich.

No. 742 (m.90d), D.d., Hil.:
Summons to render account to John Inge, custodian of Chirk. (E.159/109, m.216d.)

No. 743 (m.116), Br. Ret., Mich.:
Distraint of the collectors of ecclesiastical taxes (listed).

No. 744 (m.126d), *ibid*:
View of the lands entrusted to John Dene to be made before he is exonerated in his account—Bwlchdinas, Blaenllyfni, Pencelly, together with the goods and chattels of the late Roger Mortimer of Chirk.

No. 745 (m.129d), *ibid*:
William Shalford and John Aleyn are to be distrained to produce the counter-rolls of Adam Withiford's chamberlainship of North Wales. Until they do so his final account cannot be made.

No. 746 (m.132d), *ibid*, Hil.:
Distraint of the goods of the bishop of Bangor, collector of the clerical Tenth.

No. 747 (m.139d), *ibid*, Pascha:
Distraint of James Audley, tenant of Llandovery and the appurtenances of Glasbury in Wales, formerly of Matilda Longespee, tenant-in-chief. Cf. also E.368/106, m.106, Br. Ret., Mich.

No. 748, *ibid*:
Distraint of William Shalford for the time he was custodian of the goods of the late Roger Mortimer of Chirk.

No. 749 (m.140d), *ibid*, Trin.:
The king wants to know the annual value of the lands of Lewis de la Pole, of Roger Tyrel in Glamorgan and of Nicholas Sandeley in Llandovery. Cf. also E.368/106, m.126d, Br. Ret., Mich.

No. 750 (m.142d), *ibid*:
A day for account is given to the controller of Adam Withiford, late chamberlain of North Wales.

No. 751, *ibid*:
Ditto for the Controller of South Wales.

No. 752 (m.143d), *ibid*:
The king wishes to know the annual value of the issues of Haverford castle.

No. 753 (mm.152d and 153), St. et Vis., Mich.:
View: Adam Withiford, chamberlain of North Wales, 8 April 1330 to 31 March 1331 (but his predecessor, Nicholas Acton, handed over the office only on 14 August 1330).
Sum due: £1,352 7s. 4¾d.

No allowance can be given for expenditure on castles as the counter-rolls for the time when Roger Mortimer and John Wysham were justices of North Wales had not been delivered at the Exchequer. (Both Mortimer and Wysham were already dead.)
Consideration of these payments was adjourned and, after further allowances, he owed £168 14s. 10d.
He also owed £7 8s. 3¾d. of the remainder of the view of his account for the chamberlainship of South Wales for one and a half years. (6 Edward III and the first half of 7 Edward III; Account, S.C.6/1220/6.)
Joint debt: £176 2s. 9d.
Committed to the Fleet prison on 18 December 1332. Committed to the Tower of London in Trinity term 1334 for failure to present the counter-rolls for his period in office and died in the Tower on 15 December 1335.

No. 754 (mm. 156r and d.), *ibid*:
View: Robert Hambury, chamberlain of North Wales, 31 March 1331 to 19 April 1332.
Sum due: £1,152 15s. 5¾d.
Because of the death of John Wysham, former justice of North Wales, he could not present the counter-roll and other evidence.
After allowances owed £302 4s. 5¼d., but claimed that he spent £303 1s. 7d. on castles, which could not be allowed for lack of the counter-roll. Cf. no. 852. Account, S.C.6/1213/10. Enrolled Account, E.372/181, m.36.

No. 755 (m.156d), *ibid*, Hil.:
Account of Warin le Frere, custodian of Montgomery from 20 December 1329 onwards. (E.159/109, m.241.)

No. 756 (m.171), *ibid*, Pascha:
View of the account of John Inge, custodian of Chirk, 2 December 1331 to 2 December 1332.

E.159/109   7 Edward III   (1332–3)

No. 757 (m.101d), Recorda, Mich.:
Concerning an inquisition into the goods Edward II had in 1326 at Swansea. Cf. nos. 706, 922.

No. 758 (mm.102, 103), *ibid*:
Stephen Perot is attached to reply to the king for a debt owed to the late Roger Mortimer, earl of March. Cf. also *infra*, D.d., Mich., m.179.

No. 759 (m.107), *ibid*:
The king wants to know the accustomed fee received by the constable of Wigmore.

No. 760 (m.109), *ibid*:
Allowance to Cynfrig ap Gruffydd, sheriff of Anglesey, for money spent on purveyances.

No. 761 (m.131d), *ibid*, Hil.:
Assignment to the keeper of the New Forest of a sum from the revenues of the chamberlainship of North Wales.

No. 762 (m.166d), Fines, Mich.:
Manucaption for Adam Withiford, late custodian of Cefnllys.

No. 763 (m.236d), St. et Vis., Mich.:
Audit: Richard Symond, William Power and Henry Power of the issues of Haverford and the lands of the late Roger Mortimer of Chirk, 18 February 1331 to 26 March 1332, before they were delivered to Guy Brian; also of the lands of Laurence Hastings (a minor) in Tenby and elsewhere, 18 February 1331 to 16 November 1331.

No. 764 (m.288d), Br. Ret., Mich.:
Richard Bayston, late custodian of Denbigh, summoned to account for arrears.

E.368/106 8 Edward III (1333–4)

No. 765 (m.37), Recorda, Pascha:
William Islip, custodian of the temporalities of the priory of Carmarthen (in the king's hands due to the failure of the prior to account), is himself put in the Fleet prison for failure to account. (E.159/110, m.150.)

No. 766 (m.64), Fines, Mich.:
Thomas Clonne, custodian of Chirk, released from the Fleet prison on manucaption. (E.159/110, m.185d.)

No. 767 (m.79d), D.d., Mich.:
Respite of Robert Hambury's account until Hilary. Cf. also E.159/110, Br. d. Bar., Mich., m.161d (and D.d., Mich., m.205d).

No. 768 (m.130), Br. Ret., Mich.:
The following are to be distrained to account (cf. nos. 769–72): John Benet for Monmouth castle.

No. 769:
John Langton and Richard Wolf for the Despenser lands in Gower.

No. 770:
Robert Singleton, receiver of Gower for the same.

No. 771:
Llywelyn Du ap Gruffydd ap Rhys for Dryslwyn, Dynefwr, and Cantrefmawr.

No. 772:
The prior of Carmarthen and Thomas Duyn distrained for the chamberlain-ship of South Wales.

No. 773 (m.132d), *ibid*:
As above (cf. no. 772). The counter-rolls of the prior's account to be sent to the Exchequer.

No. 774 (m.135), *ibid*:
Order to distrain Owain ap Gruffydd ap Gwenwynwyn to pay the relief on his lands.

No. 775 (m.136d), *ibid*:
Order to distrain the dean and chapter of Bangor, collector of the clerical Tenth. (1320.)

No. 776 (m.137), *ibid*:
Philip Stoke and William Islip are distrained to render account for the temporalities of the priory of Carmarthen. Cf. also E.368/107, Br. Ret., Mich., m.122d.

No. 777 (m.145d), *ibid*, Pascha:
Writ of the king to the justice of Wales: the king had committed the custody of Caerphilly castle on 30 December 1326 to Roger Chandos together with the custody of all the goods and chattels of Edward II in the castle to answer at the Exchequer. Chandos was unable to account for them because John Felton, then custodian of the castle, previously held it against him and refused to let him enter until on 1st November Roger Northburgh, bishop of Coventry and Lichfield, came together with William Zouche and John Langton, and Chandos entered the castle only after a siege lasting until the feast of St. Gregory. The king asks for confirmation of this.

No. 778 (m.146d), *ibid*:
Robert Malley, controller and lieutenant of the late Roger Mortimer, justice of Wales, is to come so that an account can be made by the prior of Carmarthen, chamberlain of South Wales.

No. 779 (m.156), St. et Vis., Mich.:
Audit: prior of Kidwelly, collector of the clerical Tenth in the archdeaconry of Carmarthen in the diocese of St. David's.
Sum due: £42 6s. 3d., and he is to be distrained.

No. 780 (m.161), *ibid*, Hil.:
View: Roger Grey, custodian of Abergavenny castle through the minority of Laurence Hastings. (E.159/110, m.249.)

No. 781 (m.174), *ibid*, Trin.:
Audit: prior of Carmarthen and Thomas Duyn, chamberlains of North Wales, 29 September 1326 to 23 October 1331.
Sum due: £2,707 12s. 7d.
Allowances include a payment of £27 to Rhys ap Howel, justice of South Wales, from 30 November 1326.
After allowances and provisional respites owed £967 14s. 9½d., for which, on 28 July 1334, the attornies of the chamberlains were delivered into the custody of the marshal of the Exchequer.
It was claimed that the debt arose through the detention of the money by various officials and others. The Exchequer ordered the direct levy of £562 7s. 6¼d. from seventeen persons. Permission is granted to pay £800 of this debt by annual instalments at the rate of £40 a year. The rest of the debt was transferred to other men who owed it to the chamberlains. (E.159/110, m.262.)
After final accounting, the chamberlains owe in the Pipe Roll £1,439 18s. 3¼d. (Enrolled Account, E.372/178, m.43.)

E.159/110   8 Edward III   (1333-4)

No. 783 (m.11), Br. d. Bar., Mich.: York, 15 December 1332:
The king's valet, Richard Calewar, to have custody of the vills of Clynnog, Llanlibio, 'Geyrn' and 'Keghwyn' in Anglesey, and £10 p.a. of the issues for life for good service.

No. 784 (m.11d), *ibid*: Newcastle on Tyne, 24 April 1333:
Allowances to be made in his account at the Exchequer to Ralph Wedon, for money spent on the king's service in the Welsh March.

No. 785 (m.19d), *ibid*: Tweedmouth, 16 June 1333
The manor of Overton in Maelor Saesneg committed to Robert Shirbourn.

No. 786 (m.68), *ibid*, Pascha: Pontefract, 21 March 1333:
Permission for John Wynce, prior of Carmarthen and chamberlain of South Wales, to account through attornies.

No. 787 (m.73d), *ibid*: Woodstock, 6 February 1334:
Pardon of debt of the arrears of the issues of Haverford to Richard Symond, custodian.

No. 788 (m.87d), *ibid*, Trin.: Burstwick, 23 May 1335:
Allowance in his account of £3 to the prior of Carmarthen, chamberlain of South Wales, paid out for the expenses of the king's falconer in Wales.

No. 789 (mm.88d and 90), *ibid*: Burstwick, 22 and 23 May 1335:
Two writs of allowance to the same for expenses on repairs of castles, which are in a deplorable condition.

No. 790 (m.106d), *ibid*: York, 4 July 1334:
Inquiry into the prior of Carmarthen's claim that he could not collect the money for which he was responsible as chamberlain, because the officials answered only to the justice and controller and failed to answer to him.

No. 791 (m.134d), Recorda, Pascha:
Roger Grey and Richard Camvill' are to answer for the issues of Gower.

No. 792 (m.232), D.d., Pascha:
Richard Wolf puts John Goch or Philip Goch in his place to account for the goods which Edward II had at Swansea.

No. 793 (m.293), Br. Ret., Mich.:
List of people in South Wales to answer for debts.

No. 794, *ibid*:
Prior of Carmarthen is to be distrained for the arrears of the clerical Moiety of 1294–5 due from his predecessor, collector of the same in the diocese of St. David's.

No. 795 (m.293d), *ibid*:
The custodians of Chirk are to collect debts owed to Roger Mortimer by various Welshmen.

No. 796, *ibid*:
The executors of the bishop of Llandaff who was collector of 'the 5th penny in the mark' are to be distrained. The debts owed to the bishop on his temporalities are to be collected for the king.

No. 797, *ibid*:
Cadwgan ap Gruffydd is to answer for the late king's possessions in Swansea.

No. 798, *ibid*:
Llywelyn de Moselowe is to answer to the king for money taken from the late Roger Mortimer, Earl of March, which the earl had when he was arrested at Nottingham.

No. 799 (m.298), *ibid*:
The abbot of Valle Crucis to be distrained for arrears of his predecessor, a sub-collector of the clerical Tenth of Pope Boniface VIII.

No. 800, *ibid*:
Stephen Perot to be distrained for a debt to the late Roger Mortimer.

No. 801, *ibid*:
William Creppings to be distrained for debt to the same.

No. 802, *ibid*:
John Stephen and William Sandale, collectors of the Ancient Custom in Haverfordwest, are to be distrained.

E.368/107 9 Edward III (1334-5)

No. 803 (m.27), Recorda, Hil.:
Statement of the dues owed by the customs collectors of Haverfordwest.

No. 804 (m.77d), D.d., Mich.:
Respite in his account as chamberlain of South Wales allowed to the prior of Carmarthen. E.159/111, Br. d. Bar., Trin., m.215d.

No. 805 (m.88d), *ibid*:
Matthew, bishop of Bangor, puts Thomas Apenhurst and William Bromley in his place to account for the goods and lands of John Chiveresdon, late chamberlain of North Wales.

No. 806 (m.110), *ibid*, Trin.:
William Clyve puts John Belton in his place to account for the issues of South Wales.

No. 807 (m.110d), *ibid*:
Hugh Tyrel, custodian of Bwlchdinas and Blaenllyfni, cannot account because the Exchequer had no knowledge or record of the values of these lands. An extent of the lands is to be made. (E.159/111, m.253d.)

No. 808 (m.111), *ibid*:
A day for account is given to Thomas Wynter and Thomas Rode, bailiffs of Carmarthen, under the commission to search for concealed treasure in that port.

No. 809 (m.118), Br. Irr., Mich.:
Allowance of £20 is to be made to William fitz Warin, farmer of Montgomery castle, for expenses of repairing the castle.

No. 810 (m.126d), Br. Ret., Mich.:
The executors of John Chiveresdon, late chamberlain of North Wales, to be distrained for his arrears.

No. 811 (m.129), *ibid*:
Robert Singleton to be distrained for the issues of Despenser's lands in Gower.

No. 812, *ibid*:
Ditto, John Benet for Monmouth.

No. 813 (m.131d), *ibid*:
The dean and chapter of Bangor, collectors of the clerical Tenth, to be distrained.

No. 814 (m.132d), *ibid*:
Robert Hambury, late chamberlain of North Wales, has not satisfied the king for the arrears of his account and is to be attached.

No. 815 (m.135d), *ibid*:
Commission to the bailiffs of North and South Wales ports to prevent treasure leaving the country.

No. 816 (m.137d), *ibid*:
Further demands for accounting for arrears addressed to the Prior of Carmarthen.

No. 817 (m.138d), *ibid*:
List of South Wales debtors. (E.159/111, m.318.)

No. 818 (m.150), *ibid*:
Inquest into the results of the making of the extent of the lands of Robert Baldok and Hugh Despenser the Younger in Glamorgan and the March.

No. 819 (m.181d), St. et Vis., Trin.:
View of the account of William Ortalewe for Conway castle, 20 October 1326 to 20 November 1326.

No. 820 (m.184), *ibid*:
Audit of the account of Robert Harley of the goods of the late Roger Mortimer received in South Wales, 1 December 1330 to 4 February 1331. (E.159/111, m.284.)

E.159/111   9 Edward III   (1334–5)

No. 821 (m.6), Comm., Mich.:
Two Exchequer clerks are assigned to go to Wales to hear the account of Robert Hambury, chamberlain of North Wales, who is too busy to come. Hambury is summoned to appear before them at Caernarvon, and the clerks are instructed to bring the money to the Exchequer at York.

No. 822 (m.50d), Br. d. Bar., Hil.: Westminster, 26 September 1334:
Concerning the dispute over the manor of Accleston (Hereford) being a temporality or spirituality of Llandaff diocese. Cf. nos. 655, 830.

No. 823 (m.64), *ibid*: Privy Seal, Westminster, 26 September 1334:
Grant of £800 to the prior of Carmarthen.

No. 824 (m.83d), *ibid*, Pascha: York, 24 May 1335:
The king wants to know the terms of the charter of Montgomery castle and town. The Exchequer is ordered to examine the 'Statuti Marchie' of Henry III's reign.

No. 825 (m.93), *ibid*, Trin.: York, 3 June 1335:
Grant for good service, of arrears owed by him to Adam ap Llywelyn, bailiff of Creuddyn in the commote of 'Pernith' (Penweddig) in South Wales.

No. 826, *ibid*: Privy Seal, York, 3 June 1335:
Grant to Rhys ap Ieuan of the right to pay in instalments the amercement imposed on him by Gilbert Talbot, justice of South Wales.

No. 827 (m.94), *ibid*: Privy Seal, York, 3 June 1335:
Grants and respites for good service done by them, to Ieuan ap Gruffydd, Llywelyn ap Ieuan and m.108d) Ieuan ap Llywelyn.

No. 828 (m.96), *ibid*: York, 23 May 1335:
Grant to Rhys ap Gruffydd ap Howel of the manor of Narberth for life for good service.

No. 829 (m.98d), *ibid*: York, 10 June 1335:
The chamberlain of South Wales allowed money paid to the justices.

No. 830 (m.104), *ibid*: York, 11 June 1335:
The bishop of Llandaff made quit of royal taxes on the manor of Acclesto which is a temporality attached to spiritualities. Cf. nos. 655, 822, 910.

No. 831 (m.107d), *ibid*: Newcastle on Tyne, 2 July 1335:
William fitz Warin accounts as custodian of Montgomery.

No. 832 (m.108), *ibid*: Newcastle on Tyne, 1 July 1335:
Robert Harley is not to be burdened to account for the lands of the late Roger Mortimer of Wigmore which he had handed over to a special custodian.

No. 833 (m.108d), *ibid*: Newcastle on Tyne, 23 June 1335:
The custodian of the lands of the late Roger Mortimer of Wigmore is ordered to come to account.

No. 834 (m.114), *ibid*: Newcastle on Tyne, 5 July 1335:
Allowances to the prior of Carmarthen, chamberlain of South Wales, fo money spent on Dynefwr castle.

No. 835 (m.122d), *ibid*: Cowick, 16 May 1335:
The king wants to be certified about the debt of Henry Shirokes, late chamberlain of North Wales.

No. 836 (m.160), Recorda, Hil.:
Proceedings concerning the debt of Robert Perrers, custodian of Haverford.

No. 837 (m.182), *ibid*, Trin.:
Memorandum that Robert Hambury led 30 men-at-arms and 100 foot-soldiers to Pontefract and thence to northern parts. Also John de Vyene who was responsible for 30 men-at-arms and 1,300 foot-soldiers.

E.368/108   10 Edward III   (1335–6)

No. 838 (m.36), Recorda, Hil.:
The prior of Carmarthen is to carry out repairs on South Wales castles (E.159/112, mm.14, 14d; cf. also m.51, Br. d. Bar., Mich.)

No. 839 (m.59), *ibid*, Trin.:
The king wishes to know the value of the temporalities of the priory of Carmarthen. (E.159/112, m.172, and cf. also Br. d. Bar., Trin.)

No. 840 (m.97d), D.d., Trin.:
Robert Hambury, chamberlain of North Wales, puts as his attorney William de la Bataille.

No. 841 (m.120), Br. Ret., Mich.:
Guy Brian is to be distrained to account for Haverford.

No. 842 (m.120d), *ibid*:
Distraint of the prior of Carmarthen.

No. 843, *ibid*:
Distraint of James Audley, custodian of Llandovery and of the lands of Matilda Longespée.

No. 844, *ibid*:
Distraint of John Benet for Monmouth.

No. 845, *ibid*:
Distraint of Robert Singleton and Llywelyn Du ap Gruffydd ap Rhys for Dryslwyn and Dynefwr.

No. 846 (m.123d), *ibid*:
The bailiffs of Denbigh, Goseford, Danwelle, Conway, Beaumaris, Caergybi, Caernarvon, Pwllheli, to be distrained to account under the commission to prevent the export of bullion. Ditto to bailiffs of South Wales. (E.159/112, m.192d.)

No. 847 (m.124), *ibid*:
Two writs to distrain South Wales ecclesiastics for arrears of the clerical Tenth of 1326–7. (E.159/112, m.272d.)

No. 848 (m.126d), *ibid*:
Inquest to be made by the custodians of the goods and lands of Despenser and Baldok in South Wales. (Newport, Glamorgan, Striguil, Abergavenny, Wigmore, Castle Goodrich and Usk.)

No. 849, *ibid*:
List of distraints for debt by the steward of Pembroke.

No. 850 (m.143), *ibid*:
Richard Coggeshall, receiver of the lands of the late Roger Mortimer of Chirk, to be distrained.

No. 851 (m.148), St. et Vis., Mich.:
Audit of the account of John, bishop of Llandaff, collector of the clerical Tenth (1333–4), Llandaff diocese.
Sum due: £207 8s. 6¾d.
After allowances owes £28 12s. 7d., respited until later.

No. 852 (m.162), *ibid*, Trin.:
Audit: Robert Hambury, chamberlain of North Wales, 31 March 1331 to 29 September 1333.
Sum due: £3,606 10s. 7¾d.
After allowances owed £965 18s. 10d. for which he was committed to Fleet prison (E.159/112, m.241.) Cf. no. 754.

E.159/112   10 Edward III   (1335–6)

No. 853 (m.13d), Br. d. Bar., Mich.: Privy Seal, Cockburnspath, 23 September 1335:
Permission for Henry ap Owen, bedell of 'Manethlau' to pay his arrears in instalments because of his good service in Scotland.

No. 854 (m.14), *ibid*:
Ditto for Llywelyn Thloyt ap Rhys, bedell of Crendon.

No. 855 (m.14d), *ibid*: Edinburgh, 14 September 1335:
Ditto for Rotharach ap Ieuan ap Maredudd, bedell of Caerwedros.

No. 856 (m.15), *ibid*: Berwick on Tweed, 11 October 1335:
Ditto for Gruffydd ap Rhys ap Llywelyn.

No. 857 (m.20), *ibid*: Privy Seal, Roxburgh, 6 November 1335:
Exchequer to account with Nicholas Acton for his expenses in taking ships in North Wales.

No. 858 (m.43d), Br. d. Bar., Hil.: Knaresborough, 3 February 1336:
The prior of Carmarthen is quit of a debt of £30 owed by the men of Elfed and Gwidigada 'pro defectu cariagii maremii'.

No. 859, *ibid*: Knaresborough, 6 February 1336:
Atterminations of debts of Adam ap Llywelyn, bailiff of Creuddyn, and others (list).

No. 860 (m.50d), *ibid*: Knaresborough, 6 February 1336:
The king wants to know the amount of the clerical Tenth owed by the church of Mold, St. Asaph diocese.

No. 861 m.62), Br. d. Bar., Pascha: the Tower, 27 March 1336:
Respite of debt for Robert Hambury, chamberlain of North Wales.

No. 862 (m.210), D.d., Hil.:
Stephen Perot put as his attorney Thomas de Castro to answer for arrears due from the lands of the late Roger Mortimer.

No. 864 (m.266), *ibid*:
Llywelyn de Moselowe to be distrained to account for his custody of the money taken from the late Roger Mortimer at Nottingham. Cf. no. 798.

No. 865, *ibid*:
John Stephen and William Sandale, collectors of the customs at Haverfordwest, are to be distrained.

No. 866, *ibid*:
Ditto, the prior of Carmarthen for the arrears of the Tenth. (St. David's diocese.)

No. 867, *ibid*:
The steward of Pembroke is to distrain Stephen Perot for debts owed to the late Roger Mortimer.

No. 868, *ibid*:
William Creppings is to be distrained for debts owed to the same.

No. 869, *ibid*:
The executors of the bishop of Llandaff, collector of the clerical Tenth, in his diocese, are to be distrained for arrears.

No. 870, *ibid*:
Richard Wolf is to be distrained for the goods which Edward II had at Swansea.

No. 871 (m.266d), *ibid*:
The bishop of Llandaff is to be distrained for debts owed to Hugh Despenser.

E.368/109 11 Edward III (1336–7)

No. 872 (m.77d), D.d., Mich.:
A day for account is given to Nicholas Sardon and John Godynou, bailiffs of Conway, under their commission to survey and prevent the export of silver and treasure. (E.159/113, m.206d.)

No. 873 (m.84), *ibid*:
Richard Welles, chamberlain of South Wales, puts John le Clerk and Nicholas Hulein to account in his place.

No. 874 (m.90), *ibid*., Hil.:
The bailiffs of Beaumaris, Caergybi and Caernarvon are given a day to account under the commission to prevent the export of silver and treasure. Cf. also mm.91, 115d, Br. Ret., Mich. (E.159/113, mm.222, 225d.)

No. 875 (m.105d), Br. Ret., Mich.:
The justice of Wales to distrain Thomas Wynter and Thomas Rede, bailiffs of Carmarthen, to account under the commission to prevent the export of treasure.

No. 876, *ibid*:
The prior of Kidwelly, collector of the clerical Tenth, to be attached.

No. 877, *ibid*:
List of men to be distrained for debt by the steward of Pembroke.

No. 878 (m.131d), St. et Vis., Mich.:
Audit: prior of Carmarthen, collector of the clerical Tenth (1333) in the archdeaconry of Carmarthen in the diocese of St. David's, by John Goch, his attorney.
Sum due: £42 5s. 3d.
He has paid out and has tallies for all but £12 6s. 11d., of which £4 is allowed to him for expenses.
Owes, therefore, £8 6s. 11d.

No. 879 (m.132d), *ibid*:
Audit: Richard Welles, chamberlain of South Wales, 3 April 1335 to 29 September 1335.
Sum due: £469 7s. 0¼d.
After allowances owes 2s. 4d.
Account S.C.6/1220, nos. 8 and 9. Enrolled Account, E.372/180, m.47.

No. 880 (m.138), *ibid*:
Audit: abbot of Conway, collector of the clerical Tenth in the diocese of St. Asaph, for the levy of 1334.
Sum due: £32 2s. 7d., for which he was given a respite.

No. 880a (m.138d):
Audit: abbot of St. Dogmael's, collector of the clerical Tenth in the archdeaconry of Cardigan for the levy of 1334.
Sum due: £13 14s. 2½d., for which he is to be distrained.

No. 881 (m.138d), *ibid*, Pascha:
Audit: abbot of St. Dogmael's, collector of the clerical Tenth (1333) in the archdeaconry of Cardigan in the diocese of St. David's.
Sum due: £13 14s. 2½d. Pays nothing.

No. 882 (m.141), Recorda, Pascha:
Bailiffs of Pwllheli are attached to account under the commission to prevent the export of silver and treasure. (E.159/113, m.164d.)

E.159/113   11 Edward III   (1336–7)

No. 883 (m.29), Br. d. Bar., Mich.: Westminster, 3 May 1336:
Exoneration of prior of Carmarthen of debts of subordinates who have failed to account, as was proved on enquiry.

No. 884 (m.33), *ibid*: Westminster, 14 March 1336:
The chamberlain of South Wales is to pay Andrew Montgomery and Philip Clannon £50 for their expenses in arresting ships for the king's service in South Wales.

No. 885 (m.39), *ibid*: Stirling, 2 November 1336:
Exoneration from rent for William Irreys ap Gruffydd on his land in Iscoed by Cardigan which before forfeiture had belonged to Llywelyn ap Arthen.

No. 886 (m.60), *ibid*: Bothwell, 1 December 1336:
Grant to the convent of Carmarthen that the arrears of the debt accumulated by the prior are to be paid in instalments.

No. 887 (m.62), *ibid*., Hil.: Bothwell, 16 December 1336:
Writ of enquiry, with endorsement, as to the terms by which Philip Middleton holds the castles of Montgomery, Simondes castle and Chirbury.

No. 888 (m.79), *ibid*, Pascha: Westminster, 12 March 1337:
Allowance to men of Manorbier and Pencelly to pay the king a debt on the lands of a fugitive in instalments, 'quia prefati homines paupertate casualiter superveniente multiplicitier deprivuntur'. (E.159/115, m.338, D.d., Trin.)

No. 889 (m.97d), *ibid*: Westminster, 16 March 1337:
Arrangements for the lands of the late Edmund Mortimer during the minority of his heir.

No. 890 (m.115), *ibid*, Trin.: Stamford, 30 May 1337:
Complaint by the abbot of Tintern of unjust distraint by the sheriff of Norfolk on the abbot's manor of Acle granted to him by Roger Bigod.

No. 891 (m.174), Recorda, Trin.:
A list of debts owed to the king by Hugh Audley, earl of Gloucester, including the debts of his ancestors and of the ancestors of his wife, Margaret de Clare.
Clare debts include £368 8s. 2½d. of sums received by Hugh Audley the Elder, as justice of North Wales, and never accounted for.

No. 892 (m.194), D.d., Mich.:
The prior of Carmarthen puts John Goch in his place to render account for the clerical Tenth.

No. 893 (m.223d), D.d., Pascha:
The abbot of Aberconway, collector of the clerical Tenth, puts Henry Eccleshale in his place to render account.

No. 894, *ibid*:
Ditto, prior of Brecon and prior of Haverford put John Goch as attorney.

No. 895, *ibid*:
Ditto, the prior of St. Dogmael's puts William Hillyng or William Bromleye as attorneys.

No. 896 (m.261), Br. Irr., Mich.:
Assignment of a debt, owed to the king by the abbot of Tintern, to the Peruzzi of Florence.

No. 897 (m.279), Br. Ret., Pascha:
Writs to the collectors of clerical taxes, including Welsh dioceses.

E.368/110   12 Edward III   (1337–8)

No. 898 (mm.68, 69), D.d., Mich.:
A day for account is given to John Foder and Philip Lloyd, bailiffs of Cardigan.

No. 899 (m.85), *ibid*, Hil.:
John Valle, controller of South Wales, puts in his place to account William Blaunkeney. (E.159/114, m.221.)

No. 900 (m.91d), *ibid*, Pascha:
Griffin Cam ap David Dougan puts in his place to account Nicholas Hulein and John Clerk who will answer for 140m. raised and received from the tenants of the late Roger Mortimer, earl of March, in Cardigan, Cantrefmawr, Elfed and Gwidigada.

No. 901 (m.93d), *ibid*:
John Coky, bailiff of Beaumaris, is to render account under the commission to examine coinage and prevent the export of treasure. 29 September 1335 to 29 September 1337. (E.159/114, m.227d.)

No. 902 (m.94), *ibid*:
The bailiffs of Beaumaris and Caernarvon, under the above commission, put Henry Eccleshale as their attorney to account.

No. 903 (mm.105, 106), Br. Ret., Mich.:
The above-mentioned bailiffs and those of Caergybi are to be distrained.

No. 904 (m.114), *ibid*:
The justice is to distrain Eignon Parson, Nicholas Sardon and the heirs and executors of Matthew Ellerton for the goods of John Chiversdon, late chamberlain of North Wales.

No. 905 (m.117d), *ibid*:
List of debtors of the late Roger Mortimer to be distrained.

No. 906 (mm.144 and d.), St. et Vis., Hil.:
Audit: Richard Welles, chamberlain of South Wales, 29 September 1335 to 29 September 1337.
Sum due: £949 1s. 9d.
After allowances owed £356 5s. 9¾d. which were ordered to be levied from his possessions.
Proceedings about this debt continued, inconclusively, until 1347. Cf. no. 976.
Account, S.C.6/1220/9. Enrolled Account, E.372/181, m.34.

E.159/114   12 Edward III   (1337–8)

No. 907 (m.6), Comm., Mich.:
Henry Eccleshale is to enquire about the arrears of the clerical Tenth owed by the prior of Prestholm, collection in Bangor diocese. He is to receive the money and pay it to the king.
Cf. also E.159/114, m.220, D.d., Hil.; m.282, Br. Ret., Mich.

No. 908 (m.8), *ibid*, Hil.:
The king wants to know the amount of the debt owed to the late Hugh Despenser the Younger, by Hugh's receiver, John Bradford, in Glamorgan.

No. 909, *ibid*:
The collectors of the clerical Tenth, St. Asaph diocese, are to be distrained.
Cf. also E.159/114, m.282, Br. Ret., Mich.

No. 910 (m.15), Br. d. Bar., Mich.: Privy Seal, Westminster, 22 August 1337:
Permission for the abbot of Aberconway to pay his debt for the clerical
Tenth in instalments.

No. 911 (m.43d), *ibid*: Westminster, 2 October 1337:
Dispute as to whether or not the manor of Accleston (Hereford) is part of
the temporalities of the bishop of Llandaff. Cf. no. 830.

No. 912 (m.53), *ibid*, Hil.: Westminster, 1 September 1337:
Allowances are given in his account to Hugh Tyrel, custodian of Bwlchdinas
and Blaenllyfni.

No. 913 (m.58), *ibid*: Westminster, 3 January 1337:
Respite in his account allowed to John Montgomery.

No. 914 (mm.66, 71), *ibid*: Westminster, 17 December 1337:
Allowance in his account for £40 p.a. to Richard Welles, chamberlain of
South Wales, for this sum paid out of the farm of Lampeter and Cardigan
to Gilbert Turbervill'.

No. 915 m.66d), *ibid*: the Tower, 21 September 1337:
Allowances to the above-mentioned chamberlain for money given to men
purveying ships in the Bristol Channel for the king's services.

No. 916 (m.152), Recorda, Hil.:
A list of debts due from the earldom of Chester.
Includes a debt of 5,000 marks due from Oliver Ingham for the farm of
the office of justice of Chester, of the county of Flint, and of the castles of
Chester, Flint and Rhuddlan from 29 November 1328 to 1333, at 1,000 marks
a year.

No. 917 (m.270), D.d., Hil.:
Lodewycus de Bromfield, archdeacon of St. Asaph, and John Topan,
collector of the clerical Tenth in the diocese of St. Asaph, put Henry
Eccleshale in their place to account.

No. 918 (m.282d), Br. Ret., Mich.:
Richard Wolf to reply for the king's goods at Swansea.
The prior of Carmarthen similarly to account for the clerical Tenth of
Pope Boniface VIII, collected by his predecessor.

No. 919 (m.283), *ibid*:
Order to distrain the executors of the testament of John, bishop of Llandaff,
collector of the levy of the fifth penny in the mark.

No. 920 (m.289), *ibid*:
Writ to John Mowbray, lord of Gower, ordering him to summon Crown
debtors in Gower to the Exchequer.

E.368/111   13 Edward III   (1338–9)

No. 921 (m.10), Recorda, Mich.:
John Wroth is attached to reply for the chamberlainship of South Wales.
(E.159/115, m.222.)

No. 922 (m.35d), *ibid*, Hil.:
Record of an inquisition at Swansea on 3 October 1328 into the goods of
the late King Edward II which he had in Gower in the twentieth year of his
reign (in the autumn of 1326). The jurors declared that his various goods
(enumerated) were worth £300 in the custody of John Langton who was
summoned to the Exchequer to answer for this debt. Langton produced
royal letters patent under the privy seal, dated 3 November 1329, testifying
to the delivery of precious vessels and other objects to the official designated
by the king, and he claimed that he had thus delivered all the goods of
Edward II that he had held. A further inquisition taken at Swansea on
15 June 1339: the jurors declared that in addition to the goods thus delivered
by Langton he had detained at Swansea other possessions of King Edward II,
worth £100. Order to the justice of South Wales to levy this sum from
Langton's possessions.
(E.159/115, m.236d, Comm., Trin.; m.255, Recorda, Pascha.) Cf. no. 757.

No. 923 (m.64), Fines, Pascha:
Manucaption for John Goch for the proceeds of the alien religious houses
of North Wales for which he is due to account. E.159/115, m.247d, Recogn.,
Hil.; m.292d, Fines, Pascha.

No. 924 (m.80d), D.d., Mich.:
A day for account is given to the bailiffs of Beaumaris and Caernarvon under
the commission to examine coinage and prevent the export of treasure.
(E.159/115, m.311d.)

No. 925 (m.89d), *ibid*, Mich.:
The bailiffs of Carmarthen put in their place to account John Vale and
Henry Stratford. (E.159/115, m.316.)

No. 926 (m.93d), *ibid*, Hil.:
A day for account is given to Robert Hambury, chamberlain of North Wales.
(E.159/115, m.321.)

No. 927 (m.118), Br. Ret., Mich.:
The bailiffs of Cardigan are to be distrained under the commission to
prevent export of treasure.

No. 928 (m.136), *ibid*, Hil.:
Distraint of John Charlton for a debt of £420 7s.

No. 929 (m.153d), St. et Vis., Mich.:
Audit: abbot of St. Dogmael's. collector of the clerical Tenth, in the archdeaconry of Cardiganshire, St. David's diocese, for the second year of the Tenth (1335).
Sum due: £29 9s. 9d.
A day is given to render account. (E.159/115, m.370.)

No. 930 (m.158), *ibid*, Hil.:
Audit: John, bishop of Llandaff, collector of the biennial clerical Tenth (1335).
Sum due: £118 14s. 0½d.
And for the first year of the triennial Tenth:
Sum due: £87 18s. 4d.
Total debt: £207 12s. 4½d. (E.159/115, m.355.)

No. 931 (m.150), *ibid*:
Audit: prior of Carmarthen, collector of the biennial clerical Tenth in the archdeaconry of Carmarthen, St. David's diocese (1335).
Sum due: £84 10s. 6d.
Allowance of £42 given.
Owes £42 10s. 6d.
Paid: £1 3s. 6d.
Owes £41 8s. for which a day is given. (E.159/115, m.405.)

E.159/115   13 Edward III   (1338–9)

No. 932 (m.7), Comm., Trin.: Westminster, 24 July 1338:
Allowance to the collectors of the Welsh clerical Tenth of £85 already paid to the king.

No. 933 (m.23), Br. d. Bar., Mich.: Westminster, 24 July 1338:
Demand to the prior of Haverfordwest for the immediate despatching of the proceeds of the clerical Tenth which the king needs for urgent business overseas.

No. 934 (mm.26, 35, 123), *ibid*: Walton, 22 June 1338; Kennington, 5 October 1338; Berkhampstead, 8 April 1339:
Grants to Maurice Berkeley of the lands (listed) of John Mautravers in Wales and elsewhere.

No. 935 (mm.37d, 43d), *ibid*: Kennington, 20 October 1338:
A mandate concerning the debts of Hugh and Eleanor Despenser, the heirs of Gilbert, earl of Gloucester.

No. 936 (m.44), *ibid*: Kennington, 28 October 1338:
Custody of the castles of Blaenllyfni and Bwlchdinas is given to Hugh Tyrel.

No. 937 (m.85), *ibid*, Hil.: Kennington, 20 November 1338:
Summons to account to William Shalford and John Percebrigg, receivers of the forfeited lands of the late Roger Mortimer of Chirk, in England and Wales.

No. 938 (m.151), *ibid*, Pascha: Berkhampstead, 10 May 1338:
The bishop of St. David's exonerated from the grant of the Moiety of their wools (made by the bishops and other prelates in February 1338) because 'lane de partibus Wallie grosse sunt et modici valoris'.

No. 939 (m.318d), D.d., Hil.:
The bishop of Llandaff put John Newton in his place to account.

No. 940 (m.338d), *ibid*, Trin.:
Anthony Bache puts Henry Eccleshale in his place to account for the receipts of the clerical Tenth, St. Asaph diocese.

No. 941 (m.403), Br. Ret., Mich.:
Distraint of the bishop of Llandaff for a debt to Hugh Despenser the Younger, which the king has taken over.

No. 942 (m.405), *ibid*:
Distraint of the following to account:
The prior of Carmarthen for debt of his predecessor, collector of the clerical Tenth of Boniface VIII;
Llywelyn de Moselowe for the money held by the late Roger Mortimer at his capture at Nottingham;
The bishop of Llandaff, collector of the tax of the 'fifth penny in the mark'.

No. 943 (m.410), *ibid*:
List of Welsh men in the chamberlainship of South Wales to be exacted for debt.

No. 944 (m.411), *ibid*:
Writ to the Bishop of Llandaff to send the king the taxes needed for urgent business.

No. 945 (m.412), *ibid*:
Distraint of the prior of Priestholm, collector of the clerical Tenth (1332).

No. 946 (m.415), *ibid*, Trin.:
The sub-collectors of the clerical Tenth, Bangor and St. Asaph dioceses, to come to account.

E.368/112   14 Edward III   (1339–40)

No. 947 (m.105), D.d., Hil.:
The bailiffs of Llanstephan are given a day to account under the commission to examine coinage and prevent treasure leaving the realm.

No. 948 (m.120), *ibid*:
The like for the bailiffs of Caernarvon.

No. 949 (m.131), Br. Ret., Mich.:
The bailiffs of Caernarvon and Beaumaris are to account under the above mentioned commission. (E.159/116, m.271d, D.d., Trin.)

No. 950 (m.138), *ibid*:
Ditto, bailiffs of Denbigh.

No. 951 (m.138d), *ibid*:
Ditto, bailiffs of Conway.

No. 952 (m.139d), *ibid*:
The goods of Anian, late bishop of Bangor, are to be confiscated by the king for his arrears of the clerical Tenth.

No. 953 (m.140), *ibid*:
Order to distrain the bailiffs of Caergybi under the commission to examine coinage and prevent treasure from leaving the realm.

No. 954 (mm.141, 142), *ibid*:
List of people in South Wales to be distrained, including those liable for debts to the late Roger Mortimer of Chirk. (E.159/116, mm.325, 327.)

No. 955 (m.141d), *ibid*:
Distraint of the prior of Carmarthen for arrears as chamberlain of South Wales.

No. 956 (m.142), *ibid*:
The Steward of Pembroke to distrain the tenants of Richard Symond for the estreats of two-thirds of the manor at Wyston.

No. 957 (m.160), St. et Vis., Mich.:
Audit of the account of the abbot of St. Dogmael's, collector of clerical Tenth, St. David's diocese.
Sum due: £12 4s. 2½d. (E.159/116, m.277.)

No. 958 (m.161d), *ibid*:
Audit of the account of the prior of Brecon for the clerical Tenth in the archdeaconry of Brecon, St. David's diocese.
Sum due: £17 13s. 4d. as collector of the biennial Tenth (1335); £17 19s. 0¾d. as collector of the triennial Tenth (1336).
Joint debt: £35 14s. 10¾d.

E.159/116   14 Edward III   (1339–40)

No. 959 (m.8), Comm., Pascha:
Guy Brian is commissioned to bring John Stephen and William Sandale to the Exchequer.

No. 960 (m.37d), Br. d. Bar., Mich.: Windsor, 10 October 1339:
The king wants to know if John Goch, responsible for the forfeited goods of the alien priories of North Wales, has accounted.

No. 961 (m.88d), *ibid*, Pascha: Westminster, 6 March 1340:
Grant to Thomas Missyndene of the manor and port of Cemais.

No. 962 (m.99d), *ibid*: 4 September 1338:
Richard Welles, chamberlain of South Wales, is ordered to pay £57 6s. 8d. to Matilda, countess of Ulster, in part payment of a debt of the king.

No. 963 (m.103), *ibid*: Westminster, 10 May 1340:
The king wants to see the rolls of the constables of Chester, 'Bechestan', Rhuddlan and Flint.

No. 964 (m.103d), *ibid*: Westminster, 10 May 1340:
The king wants Domesday Book, the Book of Fees 'et alia memoranda scaccarii' examined to see on what terms the manor of Penrhos, Anglesey, was held.

No. 965 (m.112), *ibid*: Westminster, 13 May 1340:
Allowance of £52 6s. 6½d. to Richard Welles, chamberlain of South Wales.

No. 966 (m.128), *ibid*: Trin.: Ipswich, 15 June 1340:
The king wants to know the debts of the prior of Carmarthen.

No. 967 (m.133), *ibid*: Waltham, 4 July 1340:
The prior of Swansea, an alien, is restored his goods on account of poverty.

No. 968 (m.144d), *ibid*: Kennington, 24 July 1340:
Exoneration from debt of the convent of Wigmore.

No. 969 (m.154), Recorda, Mich.:
Concerning the inquest into the possessions of Edward II in Gower.

No. 970 (m.227), D.d., Mich.:
The abbot of St. Dogmael's puts John Says as his attorney.

No. 971 (m.227d), *ibid*:
The dean and chapter of Llandaff, collectors of the clerical Tenth (1335) put William Appleton and Richard Horon as their attornies.

No. 972 (m.254d), *ibid*:
A day for account is given to Robert Hambury.

No. 973 (m.264), D.d., Hil.:
A day for account is given to John Stephen, bailiff of Llanstephan.

No. 974 (m.274d), St. et Vis., Mich.:
Audit: prior of Brecon, collector of the biennial, clerical Tenth in the archdeaconry of Brecon, in 1336–7, and of the triennial Tenth granted in 1337.
Sum due: £35 12s. 3¾d., for which he was given a respite.

No. 975 (m.277), *ibid*:
Audit: abbot of St. Dogmael's, collector of the clerical Tenth in the archdeaconry of Cardigan.
Sum due: £12 4s. 2½d., for which he is given a respite.

No. 976 (m.286), *ibid*, Pascha:
Audit: Richard Welles, chamberlain of South Wales, 29 September 1337 to 6 March 1339.
Sum due: £580 1s. 6¾d.
Also allowed £356 5s. 9¾d. of clear debt on his previous account (cf. no. 906).
Joint debt: £936 7s. 4½d.
After allowances owes £94 1s. 7¼d. An assignment for £94 out of this debt is given to Henry earl of Derby.
Account, S.C.6/1221, nos. 3 and 4. Enrolled Account, E.372/184, m.39.

No. 977 (m.321d), Br. Ret., Mich.:
The steward of Haverfordwest is to take into his hands all the goods of the customs collectors there.

No. 978 (m.322), *ibid*:
Order to distrain the abbot of Valle Crucis, collector of the clerical Tenth.

No. 979 (m.326d), *ibid*:
Ditto, for the bishop of Bangor.

No. 980, *ibid*:
Ditto, for collectors of the Tenth, St. Asaph diocese.

No. 981 (m.329d), *ibid*, Pascha:
Ditto, for the abbot of Cymmer and the bishop of Llandaff, collectors of the Tenth.

E.386/113   15 Edward III   (1340–1)

No. 982 (m.72), D.d., Mich.:
A day for account is given to Henry, bailiff of Llanstephan.

No. 983 (m.78d), *ibid*:
Ditto, for Robert Hambury, chamberlain of North Wales.

No. 984 (m.82), D.d., Hil.:

John Houson, clerk of the late John Chiveresdon, chamberlain of North Wales, puts in his place to account, for the goods of Chiveresdon, William de la Bataille.

No. 985, *ibid*:

John Ellerker, put in his place to account for money received from Gascony, William de la Bataille and John Lanfranc.

No. 986 (m.85), *ibid*, Pascha:

A day for account is given to Nicholas Sardon and John Godynogh, bailiffs of Conway, under the commission to examine coinage and prevent treasure from leaving the realm.

No. 987 (m.107d), Br. Ret., Mich.:

Order to distrain the bailiffs of Denbigh, Gosford and Danewell under the above commission.

No. 988 (m.119d), *ibid*, Hil.:

The king wants to know the value of the castles, forests and lands of Narberth and 'Cordelegh'.

No. 989 (mm.127 and d.), *ibid*:

Summons to the debtors of the late Roger Mortimer, earl of March, including Llywelyn Du ap David, the former receiver of his lands.

No. 989a (m.127d), *ibid*:

Summons to account addressed to Nicholas Side, receiver of the lands of John Mautravers at Carreg Cennen.

No. 990 (m.137), St. et Vis., Mich.:

Audit: John Ellerker, chamberlain of North Wales, 2 February 1339 to 29 September 1339.

Sum due: £1,125 9s. 9¼d.

After allowances owed £86 13s. 10¼d., but paid £133 6s. 8d. on 26 January 1340 (on this and other accounts). Cf. nos. 1021.

Account, S.C.6/1213/13. Enrolled Account, E.372/184, m.46.

No. 991 (m.157), *ibid*:

Audit: Henry, bishop of St. David's, collector of the clerical Tenth.

Sum due: £250 16s.

Paid: £66 13s. 2d. to royal clerks.

Owes: £160 11s. 8d.

E.159/117   15 Edward III   (1340–1)

The membrane numbering of this roll is faulty, with a gap between mm. 229 and 300.

No. 992 (m. 36d), Br. d. Bar., Mich.: Kennington, 25 July 1340:
1,000m. assigned to Richard, earl of Arundel, out of the issues of North Wales, in repayment for a loan.

No. 993 (m. 39), *ibid*: Windsor, 28 August 1339:
Allowance to John Ellerker, chamberlain of North Wales, for transporting foot soldiers from North Wales.

No. 994 (m. 43), *ibid*: Wallingford, 20 November 1340:
Allowance to the same for payments made to the king's falconer, William Whittaker.

No. 995 (m. 71), Br. d. Bar., Hil.: Westminster, 28 March 1340:
Grant to Roger Hayton, the king's surgeon, of the manor of Aberffraw at a rent of £39 0s. 2½d.

No. 996 (m. 129), *ibid*, Trin.: Westminster, 25 June 1340:
Robert Hambury claimed that he was not responsible for the goods of Cynfrig ap Gruffydd, late sheriff of Anglesey, who had died in prison.

No. 997 (m. 171), Recorda, Hil.:
John Houson attached to reply for the goods of John Chiveresdon.

No. 998 (m. 180d), *ibid*, Pascha:
John Eccleshale and John Waltham, collectors of the Ancient Custom at Caernarvon, are attached to render account.

No. 999 (m. 225d), D.d. Mich.:
William Shaldeford, custodian of the lands of the late Roger Mortimer, earl of March, puts in his place to account Henry Eccleshale and William Bromleye.

No. 1000 (m. 321), *ibid*, Hil.:
A day for account is given to Robert Helpeston and Reginald Cam, bailiffs of Beaumaris, under the commission to examine coinage and prevent treasure from leaving the realm.

No. 1001 (m. 405), Br. Ret., Mich.:
Order to distrain the executors of the bishop of Llandaff, collector of the clerical Tenth.

No. 1002 (m. 405d), *ibid*:
Writ to John Mowbray, lord of Gower, to summon certain people for debt (listed).

E.368/114   16 Edward III   (1341-2)

No. 1003 (m.24d), Recorda, Hil.:
The king wants to know the amount of the debts in South Wales owed to the late Roger Mortimer, earl of March, and John Mautravers. (Cf. also E.159/118, m.9 5, Br. d. Bar., Pascha.)

No. 1104 (mm.42, 68), Fines, Mich.:
The manucaptors of John Chiveresdon made fine.

No. 1105 (m.44d), *ibid*:
John Goch, parson of Ponteynon, manucaptor for the prior of Llangenith in South Wales.

No. 1006 (m.5 5), *ibid*., Pascha:
Commital to prison and manucaption (by Welshmen) of Robert Hambury, chamberlain of North Wales, for arrears of £965 8s. 1od.

No. 1007 (m.62d), D.d., Mich.:
A day for account is given to the bailiffs of Conway under the commission to examine coinage and prevent treasure from leaving the realm.

No. 1008 (m.65d), *ibid*.:
Ditto to bailiffs of Caernarvon and Beaumaris.

No. 1009 (m.73), *ibid*:
A day for account is given to John Ellerker, chamberlain of North Wales.

No. 1010 (m.93d), Br. Irr., Hil.:
Assignment to John Beaumont of £1,250 os. 6d. due from the prior of Llanthony.

No. 1011 (m.98d), Br. Ret., Mich.:
List of debts owed to the late Roger Mortimer of Chirk, headed by £74 11s. 2d. owed by his receiver.

No. 1012 (m.99), *ibid*:
The bailiff of Caergybi is to be distrained to render account for money obtained under the commission to examine coinage and prevent treasure from leaving the realm.

No. 1013 (m.99d), *ibid*:
Further proceedings concerning the prosecution of John Houson, clerk of John Chiveresdon, chamberlain of North Wales, for keeping the goods of Chiveresdon after the chamberlain's death.

No. 1014 (m.102d), Br. Ret., Mich.:
The justice is not to omit on account of the liberty of the bishop of Bangor to take from the goods of Anian, late bishop of Bangor, arrears of debt owed to the king.

No. 1015 (m.105d), *ibid*:
Order to distrain on the goods of the prior of Carmarthen for arrears of the clerical Tenth, of which he was collector.

No. 1016 (m.106d), *ibid*:
John Ellerker, chamberlain of North Wales, to be satisfied for the wrongful exaction of the debt of a subordinate, Thomas Warwick, sub-sheriff of Anglesey.

No. 1017 (m.108d), *ibid*:
Robert Baxby, attorney of the bishop of Llandaff, collector of the clerical Tenth, is to be attached.

No. 1018, *ibid*:
Order to distrain the bailiffs of Denbigh, Gosford and Danewell under the commission to prevent the export of treasure.

No. 1019 (m.111d), Br. Ret., Hil.:
Order to distrain the bishop of Bangor for debt and also the abbot of Cymmer for small debts.

No. 1020 (m.113), *ibid*:
Inquest whether John Houson, clerk of John Chiveresdon, late chamberlain of North Wales, had absconded to Chester with the property of the dead chamberlain, including money owed to the king.

No. 1021 (mm.131d, 132r), St. et Vis., Mich.:
(i) Audit (vacated and incomplete): John Ellerker, chamberlain of North Wales, 29 September 1339 to 5 April 1340 (m.131d).
(ii) Audit of the same for the same period (m.132r):
Sum due: £599 19s. 0½d.
Also owes in his account as escheator in North Wales, 28 October 1338 to 12 June 1340, a further debt of 20 marks.
Joint debt: £613 5s. 8½d.
After allowances has a surplus of £196 13s. 3d.
Cf. no. 990.
Account, S.C.6/1213/14 and 15. Enrolled Account, E.372/185, m.45.

No. 1022 (m.151d), *ibid*, Trin.:
Audit: bishop of Llandaff, collector of the clerical Tenths in his diocese.
Sum due: £414 17s. 1½d.
Claims that this amount is assigned to the Acciaiuoli of Florence, the king's creditors.
Owes £6 11s. 7d., which are respited.

E.159/118   16–17 Edward III   (1341–2)

No. 1023 (m.49), Br. d. Bar., Mich.: York, 28 November 1341:
Allowance in his account to John Ellerker, chamberlain of North Wales, of money spent on the transport of troops from North Wales to Gravesend.

No. 1024 (49d), *ibid*: Stamford, 26 November 1341:
The king wants to know how much has formerly been due from the town of Carmarthen [endorsed with details].

No. 1025 (m.63), Br. d. Bar., Hil.: The Tower, 28 January 1342:
The king wants to know the amount of the farm of Carmarthen and Cantrefmawr (reply appended). Cf. also *infra*, m.229d, Recorda., Hil.

No. 1026 (m.163), Br. d. Bar., Trin.: Westminster, 7 June 1342:
John Ellerker, chamberlain of North Wales, is appointed escheator of North Wales.

No. 1027 (m.246d), Recorda, Pascha:
William Sandale completed his account as customs collector at Haverford. He has been detained in the Fleet prison.

E.368/115   17 Edward III   (1342–3)

No. 1028 (m.93d), D.d., Mich.:
A day for account is given to John Goch, parson of Ponteynon, appointed to receive the goods of alien priories.

No. 1029 (m.104), *ibid*, Pascha:
Robert Helpeston and Reginald Cam commissioned to examine counterfeit money in Caernarvonshire made Henry Eccleshale their attorney.

No. 1030, *ibid*:
Ditto, John Cokay and Adam Sandbache in Beaumaris made Henry Eccleshale their attorney.

No. 1031 (m.105), D.d., Trin.:
A day for account is given to Thomas of Castle Goodrich, chamblerlain of South Wales. (E.159/119, m.282.) Account, S.C.6/1221/3 and 4.

No. 1032 (m.121), Br. Ret., Mich.:
List of people in South Wales to be distrained for debt.

No. 1033, *ibid*:
Similar for North Wales.

No. 1034, *ibid*, and m.127d:
Inquisition into the goods of John Chiveresdon, late chamberlain of North Wales.

No. 1035 (m.124d), *ibid*:
Order to distrain John Henry, bailiff of Llanstephan.

No. 1036, *ibid*:
Summons to Robert Baxby, attorney of John, bishop of Llandaff, collector of the clerical Tenth, who has not paid his arrears.

No. 1037, *ibid*:
Order to distrain the burgesses of Llanbadarn for debt.

No. 1038, *ibid*:
Order to bring to the Exchequer Llywelyn ap David, receiver of the late Roger Mortimer, earl of March, and other debtors of the earl in South Wales (list).

No. 1039 (m.125d), *ibid*:
Order to distrain the bailiffs of Denbigh, Gosford and Danewell under the commission to prevent the illegal export of treasure.

No. 1040 (m.126), *ibid*:
The debt of John Houson is to be levied on his lands.

No. 1041 (m.131), *ibid*:
Order to distrain the bishop of St. David's, collector of the clerical Tenth.

No. 1042 (m.135), *ibid*:
Thomas Duyn, chamberlain of South Wales, is to be attached to account for arrears.

No. 1043 (m.195), St. et Vis., Trin.:
Audit of the account of William Sandale, collector of the Ancient Custom at Haverfordwest.

No. 1044 (m.197d), *ibid*:
Audit of the account of Thomas Foit of Llanstephan, collector of the wool custom between Chepstow and Chester.

E.159/119   17 Edward III   (1342–3)

No. 1045 (m.85), *ibid*, Hil.: Kennington, 28 January 1343:
Respite in his account for Robert Hambury who is attending to the transfer of Welsh troops abroad.

No. 1046 (m.104d), *ibid*: Byfleet, 17 February 1343
The rolls are to be examined to discover the correct assessment of the Tenth on Llanthony Priory.

No. 1047 (m.121d), *ibid*, Pascha:
Pardon of part of the rent to Richard, earl of Arundel on the manor of 'Kery Beytirk' in the lordship of Dolforwyn that had belonged to Edmund Mortimer.

No. 1048 (m.210), Recorda, Pascha:
Names of the deputies of the collectors of the clerical Tenth including those for Wales.

No. 1049 (m.330), Br. Ret., Mich.:
The abbot of Aberconway and the dean and chapter of Bangor, collectors of the clerical Tenth (for 1338) to be distrained.

INDEX

References to entry numbers indicated in **bold** type.

CASGLIAD LLEOL

I'W DDE
TO B

Rhif Llyfr
Book No.

Please retu
DATE STAMP
books whi
Rules & Re

Dychweler
ISOD. Codi
yn ôl is-dd

LK

070 830 540 705 28

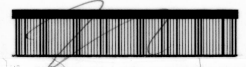